The
Global
Vegan Waffle
Cookbook

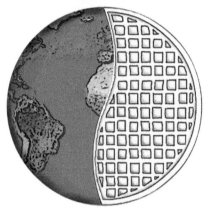

106 Dairy-Free, Egg-Free Recipes for Waffles & Toppings, Including Gluten-Free, Easy, Exotic, Sweet, Spicy, & Savory

Dave Wheitner

DIVERGENT
DRUMMER

Second Edition
Divergent Drummer Publications
Portland, Oregon

ISBN: 978-1-7374057-1-9

Library of Congress Control Number: 2021911890

Book feedback and inquiries: waffleparty.com/contact/

Divergent Drummer Publications
Portland, Oregon

This book is dedicated to a healthy, compassionate, and sustainable future for all of us.

Contents

"GF" indicates gluten-free waffles. All toppings are GF, assuming use of wheat-free soy sauce.

Introduction

Welcome to the first cookbook devoted entirely to vegan waffles and vegan waffle toppings. A great addition to the experienced chef's collection, it is also well-suited for anyone just getting into baking. Whether you're practicing or merely exploring veganism, simply find vegan waffles interesting, or maintain a dairy-free or egg-free diet for other reasons, you'll find food here that hits the spot.

This revised and expanded edition incorporates reader ideas and suggestions. I've added metric volume and weights for most measurements above tablespoons. There are more gluten-free waffle recipes using flaxseed, including gluten-free versions of several popular originals. There are some scrumptious new topping recipes and various revisions for greater user friendliness. I want as many people as possible to experience the joy of delicious vegan waffles.

You will have the opportunity to enjoy a broad range of ingredients, and to incorporate flavors where you may not be used to seeing them. For example, have you ever seen kale or basil in a vegan waffle? Recipes range from simple to complex, from sweet to savory, and from traditional to avant-garde. The index includes recipes listed under specific flour types, under individual herbs and spices, and within categories including "gluten-free" and "yeast-raised." Gluten-free waffle recipes have "GF" in their names.

To support you in your vegan waffling adventures, there is also a broad range of baking pointers specific to vegan waffles. These include descriptions of many of the ingredients and how they behave, troubleshooting techniques for quality issues, and guidance on selecting cooking equipment.

Once you've baked a few batches for yourself and your closest friends, you may wish to entertain even more. Perhaps you'll even want to leverage the vegan waffle as a mechanism of social change. The later sections include tips for planning and throwing vegan waffle events, including participation in the Global Vegan Waffle Party phenomenon. After all, it's not just about baking waffles—it's about creating a kinder, more sustainable world.

People choose vegetarian and vegan lifestyles for many reasons, including physical and mental health, environmental sustainability, human rights, animal rights, spirituality, economic justice, and reduction of global conflict. Each of us has a different set of values, priorities, and experiences. Some people begin to alter their lifestyles rapidly after a particular learning experience, while others take years as they obtain and process new information. As we open our minds to new data, and question what we had automatically accepted as truth, we often discover new and refreshing ways of living.

Growing up in a community where hunting and fishing were common pastimes, I had never considered the idea of living without consuming flesh and other products taken from animals. Seeing other living creatures injured, bleeding, and killed usually gave me a slightly ill feeling, but I believed that eating lots of them was necessary. Coincidentally, an 8th-grade science project titled "What Do Plants Need to Make Food?" took me all the way to Ohio State Science Day. I was already planting seeds for later life work, but I still had more dots to connect.

My first opportunity to spend a significant amount of time with vegetarians or vegans was during a 3,800-mile bicycle trip for a charitable cause. Our team of 25 cyclists had a limited food budget, and I often felt annoyed when the vegetarians seemed to hinder buying more "real" food like hamburgers and sandwich meat. I didn't bother to notice that the vegetarians were riding just as many miles as the rest of us, without keeling over from lack of protein or other deficiencies. At the same time, I often felt somewhat guilty while eating around them, even though they never directly commented on my eating habits.

I later worked on a large environmental public health research project, with a medical doctor who had been vegan for decades. I was surprised that someone with an extensive background in medicine and public health would maintain such a lifestyle. He didn't talk about it much, but politely answered my questions. Doing my own research, I learned more about the impacts of animal product consumption, and I soon began to change my food choices.

I initially adopted an ovo-lacto vegetarian diet, giving up meat but increasing consumption of milk, cheese, and eggs. Then, upon attending my first North American Vegetarian Society conference (Vegetarian Summerfest), I was surprised to hear so much discussion about veganism. My thoughts raced: "But isn't being vegetarian good enough? I've already taken this large step, and now I feel guilty all over again! This is becoming too difficult, and these people are annoying me."

However, the information made sense, even though I did not want to hear it at first. It became clearer that consumption of large amounts of animal products was not only unnecessary, but potentially harmful to my health. Although this contradicted most of what I had previously been taught, I considered the epidemics associated with the standard American diet: heart disease, type II diabetes, obesity, cancers, and so on. I recalled how my uncle had died from a heart attack, and how my father had undergone bypass surgery at a relatively young age. I wanted to reduce my chances of suffering the same fate.

After changing my behavior, I was able to look more seriously at other benefits of a mostly plant-based lifestyle, such as animal rights and environmental impacts. While eating so many animal products, I had felt too guilty to consider such things in depth. Who wants to imagine the suffering of a factory farm dairy cow while enjoying their favorite cheese? Recognizing that food was only a piece of the picture, I also began to reduce animal products in other areas of my life.

I gradually settled upon a mostly plant-based diet and lifestyle that balanced various considerations and was sustainable for me. The amount of animal products I consume is a fraction of what it once was. I continue to champion vegan foods and values because I believe that we need to decrease our collective animal product consumption drastically. I try to set an example that "pure" veganism is not the only option. It is not about earning a label; it is about continuous, incremental self-reflection and improvement to create a better world.

In the area of food alone, there is still much work to do, so that we can sustain the well-being of our planet, our health, and other living things. This includes the realm of baked goods, most of which do not require eggs or dairy. I hope that vegan waffles, along with the vegan food parties described later, help to underscore this point.

When we mentally and emotionally detach ourselves during the intimate experience of eating, we deny our connectedness to our world in a very profound way. This has deep psychological and spiritual implications because we may generalize this habit, and it may impact our ability to relate to others. If you or someone you care about has ever been the victim of racism, sexism, homophobia, or xenophobia, consider that these attitudes often include a sense of detachment or disconnectedness, and a "they're lesser than me" justification. This is like the attitudes that often accompany our treatment of other animals. All of us—all living, sentient beings—are in this together.

In addition to helping you create and enjoy a variety of vegan waffles, I hope that this book provides you with deeper connection, fulfillment, and integrity. Never underestimate the awesome power of a delicious vegan waffle.

Cooking Essentials

Overall, basic waffle batters and waffle iron technology are relatively simple, and most people with a desire to cook can make a waffle. Creating exceptionally good or fairly complex waffles, however, does require some knowledge, proper technique, and tools. This section will help you to understand some of the language used in this book, avoid some common pitfalls, stock your kitchen with the proper equipment and ingredients, and even improvise a bit when necessary.

Measuring & Timing Conventions

These are some of the techniques used in creating the recipes; following them will help to ensure that you enjoy the intended results. If you are using metric weight rather than volume, some items will be irrelevant.

Measurement of flour

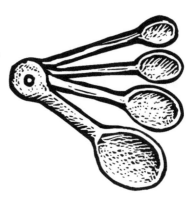

This method also applies to almond meal. Put the flour in a container large enough so you can scoop it out without having to press up against a wall of the container, because that compacts it. Stir the flour to aerate it. Scoop it out with the measuring cup or spoon so that it is filled above the top. Don't shake the cup or spoon, and don't pack the flour. Level the top by scraping off any excess with the flat edge of a butter knife. Note that different brands of the same type of flour can have different densities due to different milling practices. Environmental factors such as humidity can also affect flour behavior. Taking note of these variables when you're baking, such as writing down the brand of flour you used when a recipe came out just as you liked, can help you to replicate results in the future.

Measurement of ground flaxseed

Follow the scoop and level method for measuring flour above.

Measurement of cocoa and carob powder

If needed, sift to break up clumps before measuring. Then follow the scoop and level method for measuring flour above.

Measurement of brown sugar

Because brown sugar is naturally moist, pack it into the measuring spoon or cup, and level the top with the flat edge of a butter knife.

"Packed" ingredients

Beyond brown sugar, this term often appears alongside green leafy vegetables and herbs, including kale, spinach, and mint. It means to compress the ingredient into the measuring cup to remove most of the empty space, yielding a greater amount.

Measuring batter to pour onto the waffle iron

Each model of waffle iron has a slightly different surface area and depth, and some batters expand more than others. Thus, the directions generally recommend covering no more than two-thirds of the iron's surface with the first waffle and adjusting the amount as necessary for subsequent waffles. The first time you make each recipe, you may wish to write down how much batter is required for your iron. You might use an actual measuring cup to determine this, or you might note roughly how much you filled your favorite ladle to get the ideal waffle.

Determining cooking time

Because different waffle iron models bake at different temperatures, the recommended time provided in each set of directions is approximate. Any recipe will require some trial and error with the first waffle or two. Even if your iron has a temperature adjustment knob, a setting of "5" on one model may not correspond to the same temperature as a "5" on another. If your iron has a built-in audio timer or "done" light, you may find that it is right on the mark for some recipes, but early or late for others. For these reasons, you may wish to utilize a standalone cooking timer or stopwatch (see page 37) and record the optimal cooking time the first time you try each recipe.

If you still have the owner's manual for your waffle iron, also note any manufacturer's recommendations such as required preheating time. Just be aware that any suggested average cooking times may have been generated using non-vegan waffles without fillings. Vegan waffles and waffles with fillings may require different baking times than other waffles.

General Vegan Waffle Baking Tips

Following are troubleshooting pointers to help you climb the stairway to Waffle Nirvana.

If waffles are tough or rubbery

For non-yeasted waffles that include wheat flour, you may have overstirred the batter after adding the wet ingredients to the dry ingredients. Where directions note to "mix just until blended," the batter should still contain small lumps. These lumps don't need to be any larger than the size of a standard chocolate chip. If they're too much larger, the finished waffle may contain dry clumps. Never use an electric mixer to mix the batter; do it manually with a spatula, spoon, or fork.

Yeasted wheat-based waffle batters may require relatively vigorous mixing to break up the yeasted portion when it's blended with the ingredients added later. You can use a pair of chopsticks for this. However, you still want the batter to have small strands or lumps.

Overstirring is less of a concern for gluten-free waffles. In fact, you may need to stir longer to ensure that any large clumps of dry flour are broken up.

If waffles have clumps of dry flour

You may have understirred the batter, leaving clumps too large to absorb moisture. Again, don't be tempted to use an electric mixer; it just needs a bit more manual stirring. It's also possible that the batter didn't sit long enough. Where instructions note that a batter must sit for a specific period before baking, it's often because some grains and flours take longer to absorb moisture. Two examples are spelt and rice flour. These recipes often call for a second brief stirring prior to baking, which helps to break up any large clumps.

If waffles stick to the iron

If the waffles stick to the iron despite the waffles binding well (i.e., the iron is very hard to open), first make sure you've allowed adequate time for the iron to heat before each waffle. The batter should begin to sizzle as soon as it touches the surface, and some irons need a few moments to reestablish full temperature between waffles.

Secondly, make sure you're oiling both grids of your iron prior to each and every waffle, and using a consistently effective method to do so. This must be done even with a "non-stick" waffle iron and a batter containing oil. **It is particularly important with gluten-free waffles, spelt-based waffles, and those that incorporate ground flaxseed as a binder.** I've had the best results with a pressurized spray can of canola oil or other cooking oil. For a round iron 7 inches (18 cm) in diameter, I spray each grid for a total of 1 to 2 seconds, making 6 to 8 quick sweeps across each grill in a zigzag pattern to cover the whole surface. It may be helpful to utter, "I love ve-gan waf-fles" as you spray, with a single sweep happening on each syllable. You may eventually find that your favorite waffles don't need this much oil, but this is a good place to start.

As with any pressurized item, just be careful not to leave the can sitting right next to the heated waffle iron. It is now relatively easy to find these cans without harmful chlorofluorocarbons (CFCs). While refillable oil spray bottles eliminate additional waste, I find that they don't generate a fine enough and even enough spray for waffle irons. I also don't recommend applying oil with a brush, as a few recipe testers reported this method to yield inconsistent results with vegan waffles.

If the sticking seems to be due to the waffles not binding well enough (i.e., the waffles easily split into top and bottom halves when you open the iron), let the next one bake a little longer before opening the iron, alongside spraying the grills with oil more thoroughly. Some vegan waffles need a little longer to cook than non-vegan waffles. You may need to add 1 to 2 minutes to the time recommended in the waffle iron's directions, or to the "ready alarm" programmed into some waffle irons. This is particularly the case if the waffle contains fillings that hold moisture, such as chopped vegetables or fruit pieces. The first time you cook a particular waffle, you may wish to use a timer and jot down your preferred cooking time next to the recipe. This will reduce future guesswork.

You can also try adding slightly less plant milk or water than a recipe calls for. Between 2 tablespoons and 1/4 cup (60 ml) less is a good starting point. While this may result in a denser waffle that's not quite as moist, it may reduce the tendency to stick with some recipes. Toppings can compensate for lack of moistness.

If you're baking a yeasted waffle, double-check that you allowed the yeast to rise for at least the minimal suggested time, and that you used a non-metal bowl. Failure to follow these guidelines may result in a thinner, less-developed batter that's also more likely to cling to the iron.

Batters incorporating flaxseed as a binder can develop a greater tendency to stick if the batter sits for an extended period. Generally, batters should be baked within half an hour of preparing them. When preparing the wet and dry portions of a batter in advance for a large event (see "Food Preparation Tips," page 171), leave out the flaxseed until you combine the portions shortly before baking.

If your waffle iron is old, it's possible that the coating has pits and scratches, especially if the grills have been cleaned with abrasive or metal items. Rather than metal forks or knives, use wooden utensils like chopsticks to lift out waffles and clean out "stuck" waffle pieces—even then, scraping too hard can damage the surface. And, of course, avoid plastic utensils as they may melt and create a terrible mess.

If the above suggestions do not help, you may need a higher-wattage waffle iron. See the "Waffle irons" section (page 34) for helpful pointers.

If waffles aren't crispy enough

Begin by choosing a recipe whose description includes crispiness, as some recipes yield crispier waffles than others. Then turn up your iron's heat if it is adjustable. If the recipe calls for standard sugar, consider experimenting with a darker sweetener such as brown sugar or molasses. Try increasing the amount of sweetener by 1 or 2 tablespoons. Just keep in mind that such changes are experiments and may sometimes result in sticking or other issues.

If your waffle maker is less than 1,000 watts or is a "family size" waffle maker that spreads its energy over a large area, you may be hitting its limits (see page 34). Outside of upgrading your waffle iron, longer cooking times may be your best option.

If waffles are too soft or mushy

Whenever possible, serve waffles within 1 to 2 minutes of baking them, especially if they're yeast-raised. Otherwise, they tend to get somewhat "floppy" as they sit and cool, and you may need to put them back in the iron or toaster briefly before serving.

If the waffles seem too soft right after coming out of the iron, you may need to cook each waffle longer or bake them at a higher temperature if possible. Otherwise, when you try the recipe again, decrease the plant milk or water slightly. Between 2 tablespoons and 1/4 cup (60 ml) less is a good starting point.

If your waffles are overly done on the outside but too soft or mushy on the inside, you may need to bake them at a lower temperature.

If waffles are too dense & not fluffy enough

Baking soda and baking powder, which act to make your batter airy, start to react as soon as they get wet. Double-acting baking powder, the kind most commonly found in grocery stores for non-commercial use, does release some extra bubbles while heating. However, it works much of its magic while the batter is freshly mixed. For some batters, like gluten-free mixes, the directions include a wait of several minutes so that the flaxseed binder can develop and the rice flour can absorb some moisture. Outside of where it's explicitly directed, you generally want to bake your batter as soon as possible after you've mixed everything together. There's no exact number on this; but roughly speaking, I've had waffles turn out fine after the batter has sit for an hour, but those baked within 15 to 20 minutes of mixing are consistently better.

This is one of the reasons the yeasted waffles in the book also incorporate baking powder and baking soda: When yeast is used alone, it's important to bake a batter when the yeast is at its peak of producing air. Because environmental factors like temperature can make it tricky to time that right, I include other leaveners (baking powder and baking soda) in the same recipes as a safeguard. This way you still get the flavor of the yeast, and don't have to worry about the timing being just right for your waffles to be fluffy—unless you wait too long to bake them after adding the other leaveners.

If you have a flip waffle iron with decent wattage (see page 34), you have more leeway for thinning your batters slightly with water or plant milk. This can yield a lighter, fluffier waffle than a thicker batter. If you try this, be especially sure to spray both waffle iron grids generously with oil prior to each waffle. Add just a few tablespoons at a time of extra liquid to begin with, until you get a sense of what thickness of batter works best for your waffle iron and personal preferences.

It's also important to whisk or mix together all your dry ingredients prior to mixing them with the wet ingredients. If you don't do this, leaveners like baking powder and baking soda may not get distributed evenly throughout the mixture. Many dry ingredients tend to clump together quite quickly upon getting wet.

One trick I've occasionally used, if the first waffle in a batch isn't quite fluffy enough, is to add just a little more baking powder or, alternately, baking soda and lemon juice, to the remaining batter. (Baking powder doesn't need a separate acidic ingredient to react with it as baking soda does.) Assuming roughly 3 waffles worth of batter are left, this would be no more than 1/4 to 1/2 teaspoon of baking powder or baking soda, and up to 1 teaspoon of lemon juice if needed. Given the caveat above about making sure the leavener is evenly distributed, I do my best to sprinkle the baking powder or soda evenly across the surface of the batter with no clumps, stir it in, and then stir in the lemon juice if needed. Do be careful about avoiding clumps, as even small clumps of baking powder or baking soda can have a strong and unpleasant flavor. Also, using too much of these ingredients can give your waffles a slightly chalky overtone.

If waffles are too dry

Add 1 or 2 tablespoons of plant milk, water, applesauce, banana, or oil, or try cooking the waffles for slightly less time. However, note that thinning the batter too much or underbaking can increase the chances of sticking.

If you wish to store & reheat leftovers

While nothing beats the flavor and texture of a freshly baked waffle, you'll find yourself in situations where you simply have more batter than you can consume. Also, you may wish to make a batch on the weekend and have an easy-to-prepare breakfast for a few mornings the following week. Fortunately, you can take a few steps to optimize the quality of your vegan waffle leftovers.

Once a batter is completely mixed so that the baking powder or baking soda has begun to react with the liquid, it should be baked within half an hour or so. If stored and baked later, a batter may produce relatively dense and unleavened waffles. Thus, the best method for using extra batter is to bake it right away, put any extra waffles in a tightly sealed container or bag, and place them in the refrigerator or freezer.

If you know in advance that you'll be storing and reheating some of the waffles, you may undercook them slightly so they're less likely to burn when you reheat them. If you like them extra crispy, just bake them the normal time. If you plan to reheat the waffles in a toaster with slots smaller than a whole waffle, cut them into quarters before freezing. Cutting a frozen waffle can be difficult.

If you plan to eat the waffles within a day, the refrigerator will work for some waffles, as will the freezer. For periods of 2 days to 1 week, use the freezer. Although waffles can be stored in the freezer for many weeks, the quality may vary greatly after a week or so. Lay the waffles completely flat in the freezer so they don't take on in a warped shape that won't fit the toaster or iron.

If the toaster makes waffles too crispy for your liking, you can reheat a waffle by putting it back into the preheated waffle iron for 1 to 2 minutes. A waffle iron seals in much of the waffle's remaining moisture while heating it, whereas a toaster may dry it out a bit more.

If you're cooking for a large group

When preparing for a party or other event, try each waffle you plan on baking at least once in advance, and keep track of how long they take to bake on your iron. It's hard to overemphasize the importance of this. At our 2006 waffle party I attempted felafel waffles with little prior experimentation. Witnesses of the wrenching tragedy can probably still recall the piles of crispy waffle crumbs or "vaffeldander" I picked out of the iron. Fortunately, a few guests devoured most of them, claiming they were still delicious. I had to use a clean backup iron, and I spent half an hour restoring the other one to working condition the next morning.

The same caveat applies to the waffle iron itself. If you borrow a friend's iron, try it with your recipe in advance to see how long each waffle takes to bake, how much oil you need to spray on, and so on—don't try to determine all this the night of the party.

Yeasted Waffle Tips

Yeasted waffles require some special treatment, but they're well worth it. First, because contact with metal can impede the growth of yeast, use a porcelain, glass, or plastic mixing bowl. Secondly, yeast-based batter requires time to rise—at least 1 1/2 hours for quick-rise active dry yeast, and at least 3 hours for regular active dry yeast. Without this time, your batter may not develop properly, and the waffles may be more likely to stick to the iron. They also won't be as flavorful.

Thirdly, if the yeast is dissolved in water (or in one recipe, orange juice) that's too cool or too hot, it won't do its job. Use warm water between 105° and 115°F (41° and 46°C). You can judge this by splashing a bit onto the sensitive skin of your inner wrist—it should feel warmer than lukewarm but not hot or painful.

You can use your oven to create a warm spot for the flour mixture to rise. Make sure the oven rack is low enough for the bowl to fit in the oven. Turn the oven on for 1 to 2 minutes at 200°F (93°C). It shouldn't actually reach 200°F (93°C), but just warm up slightly. Turn off the oven, place the covered bowl on the rack, and close the oven door to keep in the warmth. If you wish to let the batter stand overnight, strengthening the yeast flavor, covering the bowl and leaving it at room temperature will work fine. Wheat flour batters may come close to doubling, while gluten-free batters will expand less.

Also, yeasted waffle batters (except for gluten-free ones) may require vigorous stirring following fermentation, when adding the final ingredients. The yeast-raised portion may develop a "stringy" consistency that doesn't easily blend with the final ingredients. Mixing with the handle end of a spoon or a pair of chopsticks can make it easier to break up the long strands into smaller clumps. You don't want the batter to be completely smooth, but you don't want too many clumpy strands larger than your pinky finger. As noted on page 36, chopsticks are great to keep on hand for several waffle-related purposes.

Finally, if you buy active dry yeast in 1/4-ounce (7 g) packets (roughly 2 1/4 teaspoons), you'll often have some left over. If you clip or rubber band the packet shut, or seal it in a food storage bag, the yeast will keep in the refrigerator for up to 4 months.

Vegan Waffle Pantry Staples

While some vegan ingredients are very common, others may be less familiar. The following information is intended to make it easier to find the ingredients, to determine which waffles you're most likely to enjoy, to discern between different varieties of the same ingredient, and to judge which substitutions are more likely to work when necessary.

If you have a favorite non-vegan recipe that you'd like to convert into a great vegan dish or vegan waffle topping recipe, the below will also provide some substitution ideas for butter, eggs, and milk taken from animals. If you can't find some of the items in your local grocery store, try to locate a local food co-op or a health foods store.

Alongside the items here, you'll want to keep a supply of the herbs and spices for your favorite waffles.

Flours, grains, & seeds utilized like flours

The recipes in this book use several types of flour. Because they have different properties, one can't always be substituted for another. Wheat flours generally have the highest gluten content, and the higher the gluten content, the greater the binding and elasticity of the waffle. Replacing wheat flour with a non-wheat ingredient may not work because the gluten content may no longer be high enough to provide proper binding or stick-togetherness—the waffles may split into two halves upon opening the iron. This is why recipes with non-wheat flours often incorporate additional binding ingredients.

While it's often safe to do the converse, replacing a non-wheat ingredient with a wheat ingredient, you may still need to adjust the liquid amount because some flours absorb more moisture than others. Additionally, different grains and seeds impart slightly different flavors.

Below are most of the flours, grains and seeds used in this book. Because ground flaxseed is utilized as a binder rather than a flour, it is discussed later under "Binders" (page 28).

All-purpose flour

Made from wheat, all-purpose flour has had some of the grain removed so it can be stored longer—unfortunately, some nutrition is also lost in this process. All-purpose flour is sometimes used alongside other flours like whole wheat to make the waffle lighter and fluffier. It can also be used alongside lower-gluten flours for additional binding. While the unbleached and bleached varieties will yield similar results, the unbleached flour involves less chemical processing.

Almond meal

Almond meal is made by grinding the entire almond, including the skin. Almond flour is made by blanching the almond to remove the skin before grinding it. Almond meal is a little coarser than almond flour. I prefer the texture of almond meal and call for that in recipes, but you can use either. Some companies use the terms *almond meal* and *almond flour* interchangeably.

Amaranth flour

Amaranth's colorful tufts produce thousands of tiny spherical seeds with a high protein content. The whole seed can be cooked in water and served warm as a breakfast cereal, or it can be ground into flour. Because the seed is so small, be careful not to confuse amaranth flour with non-ground amaranth seed.

Buckwheat flour

Despite the name, it is not related to wheat. If you're making waffles for someone with gluten or wheat sensitivities, be sure to get pure buckwheat flour that hasn't been cross-contaminated with wheat. Because some find the flavor of buckwheat flour overpowering, it is often used alongside a milder flour.

Cornmeal

Cornmeal is simply ground corn. Because it doesn't have sufficient binding properties on its own, it is used alongside flours and binders to create a crispier, slightly coarser texture, and a more toasted flavor. It should not be confused with corn flour, which is ground more finely and therefore behaves differently.

Hempseed

The Mucho Molassesey Vegan Power Waffles (page 118) use ground hempseed, also called hemp protein powder. Individuals engaging in above-average levels of athletic activity sometimes use it as a nutritional supplement. Thus, it is often carried in the nutritional supplements section of food and fitness stores. While large containers of ground hempseed can be relatively expensive, envelopes containing a few tablespoons are available.

Oats

This book references several forms of this common grain. Oats may be ground into flour. They may be chopped into small pieces with blades to form Irish or steel cut oats. They can be steamed and rolled into small, flat ovals to be sold as rolled oats. "Quick oats" are rolled oats that are sliced thinner and processed more so they soften and cook faster. While quick oats can be substituted for standard rolled oats, they won't provide quite the same chewy texture that the less processed rolled oats will provide. Beyond this, the different forms of oats may not be used interchangeably without making other recipe adjustments.

Quinoa seed and flour

Pronounced "kee-NO-ah" or "KEEN-wah," the whole quinoa seed cooks similarly to grains, contains all the essential amino acids, and has a slightly nutty flavor. It is usually, but not always, processed to remove the saponin, a bitter substance coating the exterior. Place a few pieces on your tongue before cooking it or adding it to batter. If you detect a strong bitterness, do the following just before cooking: place it in a fine mesh strainer, rinse under cold water for 1 to 2 minutes, and drain. Because quinoa is relatively expensive in flour form, only one recipe in this book calls for it alongside the whole non-ground seed. (The flour form should never be rinsed!)

Rice flour

Many of the gluten-free waffle recipes call for brown rice flour. Brown and white rice flour are generally interchangeable, but there are some differences. Brown rice flour has a higher nutritional content because it includes parts of the grain that are stripped away from white rice. Partially because of that, brown rice flour has a shorter shelf life. Brown rice flour also has a nuttier flavor and a different texture.

While I enjoy waffles made with brown rice flour, feel free to experiment to see what you like best. Some people prefer a blend of the two types.

Spelt flour

Related to wheat, spelt is not suitable for many people with wheat sensitivities, but some people who cannot digest wheat can digest spelt. It has less gluten and creates waffles slightly less dense than those made with whole wheat flour. Because spelt takes a little time to absorb moisture, recipes calling for it suggest letting the batter stand for a few additional minutes before baking.

Tapioca flour

Sometimes also called tapioca starch, this fine white powder is from the root of the cassava plant. It is often used alongside rice flour to aid thickness and chewiness in gluten-free recipes.

Teff flour and whole grain teff

If you've ever eaten in an Ethiopian restaurant, you've probably had a flat crepe-like bread called injera, which incorporates teff flour. It has a somewhat nutty flavor, is gluten-free, and adds a bit of crispiness to waffles. Non-ground, whole grain teff is even smaller than non-ground amaranth, but not as fine as teff flour. Because teff flour and whole grain teff have different baking properties, be careful not to confuse them.

Whole wheat flour

This has more nutritional value than all-purpose wheat because it includes all parts of the grain. It has a high gluten content compared to the non-wheat flours listed here, so it binds well compared to other flours. The recipes here call for basic whole wheat flour. While flour labeled as "white whole wheat flour" will yield similar results, anything labeled as "whole wheat bread flour" or "whole wheat pastry flour" will yield a slightly different product. The latter two varieties have different levels of gluten, resulting in different levels of binding and chewiness.

Leaveners

In vegan waffle recipes, baking powder and baking soda provide plenty of leavening without eggs. Recipes using baking soda will also generally have an acidic item to react with it, such as vinegar, lemon juice, lime juice, molasses, brown sugar, dairy-free yogurt, or applesauce.

As for yeast, you can use either the regular or quick rise active dry yeast that comes in 1/4-ounce (7 g) packets, or in 4-ounce (113 g) jars. Alongside making the batter rise, the fermentation adds flavor and texture to the waffle. For recipes here, the regular active dry yeast requires 3 hours minimum rising time compared to 1 1/2 hours minimum rising time for the quick rise variety.

Binders

In recipes that are based upon high-gluten flours such as wheat, and that contain few or no fillings, the flour itself usually provides plenty of binding or "stick togetherness." Baking powder, bananas, and applesauce can also add smaller levels of binding. For waffles that use low-gluten or gluten-free flours, or that incorporate a large volume of flavorful fillings, additional binding may be necessary. This is why many of the recipes incorporate ground flaxseed or xanthan gum.

You can purchase pre-ground flaxseed, sometimes labeled as flaxseed meal, or you can purchase it whole and grind it as finely as possible with a coffee grinder. Once ground, the shelf life of flax shortens considerably. If grinding yourself, refrigerate any unused portion in a sealed container, and use within a week. Otherwise, follow the storage directions on the label, as some pre-ground flaxseed is prepared in a way that extends the shelf life. Ground flaxseed also has other uses—some people put it on their breakfast cereal as a source of ALA (alpha-linolenic acid, of the omega-3 fatty acid family).

Xanthan gum powder serves both a thickening and binding function, and is used in several of the gluten-free recipes. It also adds a creamier texture to the ice cream recipes. Created by allowing bacteria to ferment sugars, it is sold as a powder. Because only 1 to 2 teaspoons (or less) are required for 4 waffles, an 8-ounce (227 g) bag lasts a very long time.

If, after practice, you come to prefer the taste or texture of one binding ingredient better than the others, you may wish to experiment with substitutions. Things may not turn out perfectly at first because each binder behaves differently, but you'll move even closer to Vegan Waffle Nirvana in the long run!

Plant milks

Most recipes in this book were created with plain, unsweetened soy milk. Where a recipe calls for plant milk, you can also use moderately sweetened soy milk or another plant milk, such as almond milk, hazelnut milk, oat milk, rice milk, hempseed milk, or coconut beverage. However, because plant milks differ in composition, including protein content, fat content, sweetness, and thickness, their baking properties differ somewhat. You may need to adjust the amount slightly or try a few types or brands to see which one yields the results you prefer.

Coconut-based plant milk intended for drinking and pouring over cereal, or coconut beverage, is thinner than full-fat coconut milk. Where a recipe calls for plant milk, it is okay to use coconut beverage. Where a recipe calls for full-fat coconut milk, it's important to use that. Otherwise, the fat content of the waffle may be too low for it to bake properly. Full-fat coconut milk is also thicker than "light" varieties of coconut milk, which usually have a higher water content. Coconut cream is the thickest variety of coconut milk and can be useful for whipped cream toppings.

Sweeteners

This section is not exhaustive; it covers a few important aspects of the most common sweeteners in this book. These ingredients not only alter the flavor of the waffle, but also add caramelization and crispiness to the exterior.

Sugar

The recipes in this book calling for sugar were created with granulated unrefined or raw cane sugar. Sucanat, demerara, and turbinado sugars will yield similar results where only 1 or 2 tablespoons are required. For larger amounts, slight differences in darkness and flavor may occur. Refined white granulated sugar will also work, but some vegans prefer to avoid brands that filter their sugar through charred animal bone as part of the refining process. If you're baking for vegan friends and don't know where they stand on this, it's safest to ask or just use an unrefined sugar.

Maple syrup

This refers to genuine maple syrup. However, it does not have to be the "grade A" variety. In fact, the recipes in this book were created with a less refined and often less expensive version sold as "grade B." When baked into items, there's no noticeable difference; and when used in toppings, the difference is slightly noticeable. Some people prefer the flavor of grade B syrup over grade A. Artificially flavored syrups may closely approximate the flavor but may yield noticeable differences in some recipes.

Molasses

Blackstrap molasses is the darkest and strongest tasting molasses. It was used in creating the recipes in this book. However, many grocery stores don't carry it, and some people don't like its bitter overtones. Medium (sometimes sold as dark or full flavor) molasses works well and has a sweeter and more subtle flavor. For the sweetest and most subtle flavor, use light or mild flavor molasses.

Sweetener substitution guidance

Because each recipe is different, it's difficult to provide hard and fast rules regarding sweetener substitutions. Nonetheless, I offer a few words of guidance.

In some waffle recipes, the slight acidity of molasses and brown sugar serves an important function: it reacts with baking soda to help provide leavening. If you replace one of these sweeteners in a recipe that includes baking soda, and there's not another acidic ingredient present, mix 1 teaspoon of lemon juice or cider vinegar into the batter just before you start baking.

Substituting liquid for solid sweeteners, and vice versa, may require slight adjustments to the amount of water or plant milk in the recipe.

While I don't have extensive experience with sugar-free sweeteners, I have achieved good substitution results in several experiments with recipes in this book. Because sugar substitutes continue to evolve, I'll offer guidance in choosing one rather than suggesting a specific type or brand. Beyond providing sweetness, sugar serves at least two other important functions in waffles. It increases browning and caramelization, and it provides structure. The better a substitute is at emulating these baking qualities, the better the results you will achieve. The acidity caveat above applies to sugar-free sweeteners—even if a substitute is designed to emulate the flavor of brown sugar or molasses, it may not emulate its natural acidity. Toppings that utilize heating to induce caramelization or thickening may also require experimentation.

If you prefer fruit-based sugar, a mashed ripe banana will often work as a replacement for other sugar in a mildly sweet (i.e., not using more than 2 or 3 tablespoons of sugar) waffle recipe. Because ripe bananas have a nearly neutral pH, the acidity caveat above applies if you're replacing brown sugar or molasses.

Oil & vegan butter

These ingredients provide fat to enhance moistness, increase flavor, improve the cooking process, and lessen sticking. Unlike their non-vegan counterparts such as dairy butter, they have no cholesterol. Canola oil has a relatively neutral flavor and works well. Olive oil, avocado oil, safflower oil, or a vegetable oil mix are just a few other options. Olive oil has light (sometimes called "pure" or "regular") varieties that have a more neutral flavor, if you prefer that.

The majority of waffle recipes in this book simply call for "canola or other vegetable oil." Some savory waffles call for "olive or other vegetable oil," because I thought the olive flavor blended well with the other ingredients. However, you're free to explore and use whatever vegetable oil works best for you.

The internet has many opinions on which oils are healthiest, which are the most environmentally friendly, and how much an oil's smoke point matters. (Smoke point is the temperature at which an oil starts to degrade, becoming less flavorful and potentially unhealthy.) The research on these topics continues to evolve, so I don't make recommendations here based upon such criteria.

Some toppings call for vegan butter. "Whipped" butters may require slightly larger amounts because they may yield less when melted. If you attempt to substitute an oil in place of vegan butter, note that the latter solidifies as it cools and often has non-oil ingredients that change its behavior. An example of such an ingredient is lecithin, which helps to keep other ingredients in a mixture from separating. Even if you use an oil that solidifies as it cools, like coconut oil, it may behave differently than vegan butter in a recipe. Or, it might work well—this can be difficult to predict. Also, because vegan butter usually contains salt, you may need to add salt if using an oil in its place.

While applesauce can replace oil in some types of baking recipes, it is often difficult to prevent sticking with an entirely oil-free vegan waffle. One exception is a waffle using a significant volume of coconut milk, which also has a high fat content.

As noted under "General Vegan Waffle Baking Tips" (page 17), it is important to oil both waffle iron grids prior to each waffle, even with a non-stick waffle iron and a batter containing oil. For this, a pressurized spray can of vegetable oil blend, canola oil, coconut oil, or other plant-based cooking oil is a good option. Brushing on oil yields less consistent results, probably because it is more difficult to achieve full and even coverage.

While many brands of pressurized spray oil have eliminated the environmentally-unfriendly chlorofluorocarbons (CFCs), I have tried the refillable oil spray bottles in an attempt to be even more environmentally friendly. Unfortunately, the ones I've tried didn't produce a fine enough mist to coat the iron evenly and sufficiently. Your mileage may vary.

Vegan cream cheese & sour cream

While the hydrogenated versions of vegan cream cheese will result in slightly firmer baked goods, the recipes here were created with the healthier non-hydrogenated versions. Some stores keep these products alongside the dairy cream cheese and sour cream, while others group them with other dairy-free items.

Cocoa powder

Two primary types of cocoa powder are widely available: Dutch-process cocoa, also called alkalized cocoa powder, and natural or unsweetened cocoa powder. Dutch-process cocoa has been treated to neutralize its acidity, giving it a mellower flavor that some people prefer. Natural or unsweetened cocoa still has its acidity and thus retains a different range of flavor overtones. As a matter of personal preference, I often use a blend of the two.

Natural cocoa reacts with baking soda to create a rising effect in baked goods, while Dutch-process cocoa does not. However, in this book, chocolate waffle recipes utilize other acidic ingredients (including brown sugar and molasses) and baking powder (which does not need an acid to react with it) alongside baking soda. Therefore, for recipes in this book, use whichever cocoa variety or blend suits your taste buds.

Peanut butter

The recipes in this book were created with salted peanut butter. However, if you normally prefer unsalted peanut butter, using that may yield results more closely aligned with your preferences.

Other not-so-common ingredients

Nutritional yeast

This deactivated yeast is grown on molasses, and it adds a rich, savory, cheese-like flavor in conjunction with other ingredients. It is sold in the form of thin, tan flakes, and sometimes as a powder, often in the bulk food section of co-ops and natural food stores. Some brands are fortified with vitamin B12.

Miso

Made by fermenting ingredients such as soybeans, chickpeas, or rice, this paste has a strong, savory, salty flavor. It is probably best known for its use in miso soup, and it plays an important role in some of the recipes with cheese-like overtones.

Carob powder

Derived from the pods of the carob tree, this rich-tasting ingredient is often suggested as a substitute for chocolate, although it has a noticeably different flavor. It does not contain stimulants as cocoa does and is a bit sweeter. Like cocoa, it is often sold in powdered or chip form. The recipes here call for toasted carob powder, which has a different flavor than raw carob powder. However, this is a matter of personal preference, so you could substitute the raw version if you like it better.

Waffle Irons & Other Essential Equipment

You don't need a super-fancy waffle maker to get started making delicious vegan waffles. However, certain waffle maker features can make a big difference in waffle texture and flavor. While I don't endorse particular brands or models here, I provide general suggestions for finding the tools that best suit your preferences.

Waffle irons

Without a waffle iron, you are limited to pancakes. A common question is, "How much should I spend on a waffle iron?" Great waffle irons can be found across a broad range of prices, depending upon the features and quality. Because models change frequently and quality is not always directly related to price, you'll need to do some research. Here are some of the features to consider:

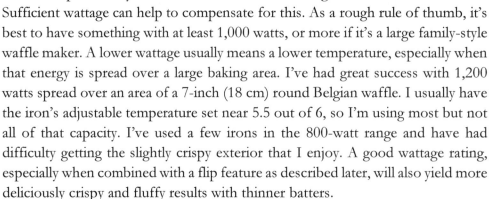

Wattage

Vegan waffles in general can take a bit longer to cook, and this is particularly the case with waffles with fillings. Sufficient wattage can help to compensate for this. As a rough rule of thumb, it's best to have something with at least 1,000 watts, or more if it's a large family-style waffle maker. A lower wattage usually means a lower temperature, especially when that energy is spread over a large baking area. I've had great success with 1,200 watts spread over an area of a 7-inch (18 cm) round Belgian waffle. I usually have the iron's adjustable temperature set near 5.5 out of 6, so I'm using most but not all of that capacity. I've used a few irons in the 800-watt range and have had difficulty getting the slightly crispy exterior that I enjoy. A good wattage rating, especially when combined with a flip feature as described later, will also yield more deliciously crispy and fluffy results with thinner batters.

Manual temperature control

This is optional but is useful for increasing the heat for waffles that are crispier on the outside and moister on the inside—or for decreasing the heat to cook the outside and inside more evenly.

Built-in audio timer alarm or "done" light

This can be handy in lieu of an external cooking timer (see page 37). Note that some recipes may require more or less time, especially if they include many fillings. A few tries will yield a sense of how long to leave waffles in the iron following the signal. Some built-in timers may not work properly with waffles that don't fill the entire iron, e.g., if there's just enough batter remaining at the end to make half of a waffle.

Rotating or flipping grill

This feature allows you to "flip" the waffle as it begins to cook, helping the waffle to cook more evenly on both sides and making it slightly fluffier. While not absolutely necessary, it can make a noticeable difference, especially around the edges of the waffle. Flip irons seem to do a much better job with thinner batters, which can yield a wonderfully light and crispy waffle. On a non-flip iron, thinner batters don't brown as well on the top side, because the batter doesn't fully contact the top grid until it's had some time to bake and rise. Flip irons, alongside helping to create air pockets in the batter with the initial flip, get both sides browning right away. Just keep in mind that more moving parts sometimes means more opportunity for things to wear out or break, so be sure to consult some reviews of any model you're considering.

Overflow catch tray

This can save a lot of time and hassle, as it will keep boiled-over batter and oil from flowing all over the counter. Dried batter can be a chore to scrape off. A cookie sheet can also serve as a catch tray.

Round versus square waffles, and depth of waffle holes

These are both a matter of personal preference. However, deeper holes hold syrups and toppings better.

If you're on a limited budget

While new waffle irons span a large range of quality and prices, used irons are also relatively easy to find. This may be because they are a popular gift item. Many people use their gifts only a few times, put them away in storage, and pull them back out several years—or even decades—later. If there are no thrift stores or upcoming moving sales nearby, a few neighbors or friends probably have an iron they'd be happy to lend—or perhaps even sell.

The basic technology of waffle irons hasn't changed much over the years. An older iron in great condition will bake a waffle in roughly the same manner as a brand-new iron, minus the advantages added by modern features such as a rotating grill. However, there are potential "wear and tear" items to look out for on used irons. These include faulty electrical cords and worn-off nonstick coating. Both of these wear out over time regardless, but the latter can be hastened if the owner used objects like metal forks to scrape out stuck-on waffles, or metal cleaning brushes. Although it's important to spray the grids with oil prior to each waffle anyway, an intact nonstick surface still helps.

Ladle

Often used for soup and punch, this tool is also handy for getting the batter from the bowl into the iron with minimal spilling. It also provides a relatively easy way to measure the batter consistently.

Whisks, spoons, & spatulas

Wire whisks are handy for breaking up powdery clumps in the dry ingredient mixture, before adding the wet ingredients. This is particularly the case with cocoa and carob. Whisks are also great for breaking up clumps of peanut butter, miso, avocado, banana, softened vegan butter, and sometimes baking powder and baking soda.

For the final mixing, using a large spoon or a spatula (rubber or silicone) rather than a whisk can help to avoid overstirring. Especially with wheat flour batters, attempting to remove every little lump can create tough waffles. Spoons and spatulas are also helpful for folding in "filling" ingredients such as nuts near the end of stirring.

Chopsticks: Waffle rescuers & yeast batter stirrers

Wooden chopsticks are useful for lifting waffles out of the iron, with a lower risk of scratching the non-stick surface than metal forks pose. For very moist and cakelike waffles, using two chopsticks to lift out a waffle (pretend you're a mini forklift) makes it easier to remove without breaking it into small pieces. In cases of sticking, chopsticks fit into the crevices of the grid to coax out stubborn pieces. Just keep in mind that you can still harm the nonstick surface if scraping too hard.

As a stirring tool for yeast-raised recipes, chopsticks help to break up and incorporate the thicker and stringier yeast-raised portion into the ingredients added later. A chopstick with a damp rag or paper towel wrapped around the tip is useful for cleaning the iron's grids occasionally.

Mashers

Several of the recipes call for thoroughly mashed banana, avocado, or potato. While a metal fork will do the trick, a potato masher will save time and effort in removing most of the lumps.

Graters & grinders

A handheld metal grater with relatively large holes, which may be sold as a cheese grater, may be used for carrots and fresh ginger. A food processor with a grating disc will also do the job. Graters with much smaller holes, sold as graters/zesters, microplane graters, or nutmeg graters, may be used for fresh ginger or nutmeg. Coffee bean grinders are useful for grinding flaxseed and may be used to prepare freshly ground versions of certain spices such as cumin.

Timers

Even if an iron has a built-in "done" alarm, it may be more accurate for some types of waffles than others. This is where adjustable timers with displays are useful. A digital cooking timer, wind-up spring powered timer, watch timer, smartphone timer, or stove or microwave timer will do the trick. Just try not to get waffle batter on your watch or phone! Some waffle makers now have built-in timers with displays or other features.

For waffle parties, I use 2 digital cooking timers that allow me to set a particular countdown time, and then stop and automatically restart at that same time with 2 simple button presses. This makes it easier to keep track of waffles in multiple irons. They also beep continuously until "stop" is pressed, unlike the 4 or 5 beeps of the irons' built-in timers that can be missed if I leave the kitchen temporarily. That can happen when cooking during a party.

Ice cream maker

This is not required for making waffles, but is needed for 3 of the sweet toppings in this book. As with waffle makers, many models exist across a broad price range. If you don't plan on making enough vegan ice cream or sorbet to justify the investment, simply purchase a pre-made frozen dessert to accompany your waffles whenever you crave a cold treat.

Batter bowls

It's important to have at least one large and one medium mixing bowl for making waffle batter. For yeasted waffles (see also "Yeasted Waffle Tips" on page 23), non-metal materials such as porcelain, glass, or plastic are best. For preparing wet and dry portions ahead of time, bowls with sealable lids may be helpful.

Also available are "batter bowls" with a handle and a pouring spout. They often have measurement lines that may or may not be accurate enough for initial ingredient measurement, but it's still necessary to use visual estimation when pouring the batter into the iron. Make sure the bowl is dishwasher-safe if you don't plan to wash it by hand. (I learned this the hard way, after the dishwasher's heat created little cracks in mine.)

Flour sifter or fine wire mesh strainer

Some recipes call for cocoa powder or carob powder, both of which can develop clumps. Vigorously stirring the dry ingredients with a wire whisk, adding the wet ingredients, and then breaking up any remaining clumps with a spoon or spatula is often sufficient. Alternately, you can sift the cocoa or carob powder and flour together, through a flour sifter or fine wire mesh strainer, after measuring them. This will reduce clumping even more.

A sifter or fine wire mesh strainer can also be useful if you wish to sprinkle a thin and even layer of cocoa powder, carob powder, or powdered sugar across the surface of a waffle.

Neutral Waffles

These recipes rely upon a variety of grains, sweeteners, and yeast for much of their taste. While always flavorful, they are intended to be consumed with toppings, and are subtle enough to work with a broad range of flavors—sweet or savory. This versatility makes them ideal for events where many toppings are present. The simpler recipes, like the Naked Vegan Waffles (page 41), are great if you're already extremely hungry or are otherwise short on preparation time. Those with a few more steps or ingredients, like the Yeast-Raised Waffles (page 43) or the Crispy Cornbuck Waffles (page 56), add specialness to a meal or celebration.

Naked Vegan Waffles

Makes 4 (7 in. or 18 cm) round Belgian waffles

A few visitors to waffleparty.com requested a very simple, neutral waffle recipe to accompany the more adventurous recipes. This easy but still tasty treat has proven to be quite popular. For a minimalist approach, simply drizzle with melted vegan butter and warm maple syrup. Or, get crazy and spoon on some Black Bean-Mango Tango (page 155).

> 1 1/2 cups (210 g) whole wheat flour
> 1 cup (145 g) all-purpose flour
> 2 teaspoons baking powder
> 1 teaspoon baking soda
> 1 teaspoon salt
> 2 1/4 cups (530 ml) soy milk or other plant milk
> 1/4 cup (60 ml) canola or other vegetable oil
> 3 tablespoons brown sugar

Combine the whole wheat flour, all-purpose flour, baking powder, baking soda, and salt in a large bowl and stir with a whisk. Thoroughly mix the plant milk, oil, and brown sugar in a medium bowl. Pour the wet mixture into the flour mixture and stir just until blended.

Preheat the waffle iron according to the manufacturer's directions. Spray both grids generously with oil. Pour or ladle the batter into the center of the iron, covering no more than two-thirds of the iron's surface for the first waffle. Adjust the amount as needed for subsequent waffles. Bake each waffle for 3 to 5 minutes, or until it can be removed easily.

Tropically Tanned Naked Waffles

Makes 4 (7 in. or 18 cm) round Belgian waffles

These exude a bit more crispiness and sweetness than the Naked Vegan Waffles (page 41), and the molasses overtones add a hint of complexity. For a true tropical flavor, pour on some Very Coconutty Syrup (page 130).

> 1 1/2 cups (210 g) whole wheat flour
> 1 cup (145 g) all-purpose flour
> 2 teaspoons baking powder
> 1 teaspoon baking soda
> 1 1/4 teaspoons salt
> 2 1/4 cups (530 ml) soy milk or other plant milk
> 1/4 cup plus 2 tablespoons (90 ml) canola or other vegetable oil
> 1/4 cup (46 g) brown sugar
> 2 tablespoons molasses

Combine the whole wheat flour, all-purpose flour, baking powder, baking soda, and salt in a large bowl and stir with a whisk. Thoroughly mix the plant milk, oil, brown sugar, and molasses in a medium bowl. Pour the wet mixture into the flour mixture and stir just until blended.

Preheat the waffle iron according to the manufacturer's directions. Spray both grids generously with oil. Pour or ladle the batter into the center of the iron, covering no more than two-thirds of the iron's surface for the first waffle. Adjust the amount as needed for subsequent waffles. Bake each waffle for 3 to 5 minutes, or until it can be removed easily.

Yeast-Raised Waffles

Makes 3 to 4 (7 in. or 18 cm) round Belgian waffles

These have a flavor reminiscent of sourdough bread, and a thin, crispy crust that's missing from most waffles. Because the batter needs time to rise, begin at least 3 hours in advance of baking or 1 1/2 hours in advance if you are using quick-rise yeast. Spoon on some fruit preserves and melted vegan butter.

1 1/4 teaspoons active dry yeast
1 1/2 cups (350 ml) warm water (see "Yeasted Waffle Tips," page 23)
1 1/2 cups (210 g) whole wheat flour
1/2 cup (73 g) all-purpose flour
1 1/2 teaspoons salt
1/2 cup plus 2 tablespoons (380 ml) soy milk or other plant milk
1/4 cup (60 ml) canola or other vegetable oil
3 tablespoons brown sugar
1/2 teaspoon baking powder
1/2 teaspoon baking soda

Dissolve the yeast in the water in a large non-metal bowl. Let stand for 5 minutes. Stir in the whole wheat flour, all-purpose flour, and salt until well blended. Cover the bowl and place it in a warm location until the flour mixture has almost doubled (see "Yeasted Waffle Tips," page 23).

After the flour mixture has risen, combine the plant milk, oil, brown sugar, baking powder, and baking soda in a small bowl. Mix thoroughly, breaking up any clumps of baking powder or baking soda. Pour into the raised flour mixture and stir until well blended. Let stand for 15 minutes, while preheating the waffle iron according to the manufacturer's directions.

Spray both grids of the iron generously with oil. Pour or ladle the batter into the center of the iron, covering no more than two-thirds of the iron's surface. Adjust the amount as needed for subsequent waffles. Bake each waffle for 3 to 5 minutes, or until it can be removed easily.

Slightly Teffy Yeast-Raised Waffles: Reduce the whole wheat flour to 1 1/4 cup plus 2 tablespoons (193 g). After the flour mixture has risen, while adding the plant milk and remaining ingredients, add 1/4 cup (50 g) of whole grain teff.

Sweet Yeast-Raised Waffles

Makes 4 (7 in. or 18 cm) round Belgian waffles

Compared to the Yeast-Raised Waffles (page 43), these are a little denser on the inside and slightly crispier on the outside. Because the batter needs time to rise, begin at least 3 hours in advance of baking or 1 1/2 hours in advance if you are using quick-rise yeast. Enjoy with Carob Halvah Spread (page 135).

1 1/4 teaspoons active dry yeast
1 1/2 cups (350 ml) warm water (see "Yeasted Waffle Tips," page 23)
1 cup (145 g) all-purpose flour
1 cup (140 g) whole wheat flour
1 1/2 teaspoons salt
1/4 cup (46 g) brown sugar
1/4 cup (60 ml) canola or other vegetable oil
1/4 cup (60 ml) maple syrup
1/4 cup (60 ml) soy milk or other plant milk
1 teaspoon vanilla extract
3/4 teaspoon baking powder
1/2 teaspoon baking soda

Dissolve the yeast in the water in a large non-metal bowl. Let stand for 5 minutes. Stir in the whole wheat flour, all-purpose flour, and salt until well blended. Cover the bowl and place it in a warm location until the flour mixture has almost doubled (see "Yeasted Waffle Tips," page 23).

After the flour mixture has risen, combine the brown sugar, oil, maple syrup, plant milk, vanilla extract, baking powder, and baking soda in a small bowl. Mix thoroughly, breaking up any clumps of baking powder or baking soda. Pour into the raised flour mixture and stir until well blended. Let stand for 15 minutes, while preheating the waffle iron according to the manufacturer's directions.

Spray both grids of the waffle iron with oil. Pour or ladle the batter into the center of the iron, covering no more than two-thirds of the iron's surface for the first waffle. Adjust the amount as needed for subsequent waffles. Bake each waffle for 3 to 5 minutes, or until it can be removed easily.

Pass the Buckwheat-Oat Waffles

Makes 3 to 4 (7 in. or 18 cm) round Belgian waffles

These wholesome-tasting treats allow the buckwheat's pronounced flavor to shine through. Top with a hearty helping of applesauce and maple syrup, or for an even heartier treat, spoon on some Savory Cashew-Mushroom Sauce (page 151).

  1 cup (150 g) buckwheat flour
  1/2 cup (73 g) all-purpose flour
  1/2 cup (56 g) rolled oats
  2 teaspoons baking powder
  1/2 teaspoon baking soda
  3/4 teaspoon salt
  1 3/4 cups (410 ml) soy milk or other plant milk
  1/3 cup (80 ml) smooth applesauce
  2 tablespoons brown sugar
  2 tablespoons canola or other vegetable oil
  2 tablespoons ground flaxseed
  1 teaspoon vanilla extract

Combine the buckwheat flour, all-purpose flour, oats, baking powder, baking soda, and salt in a large bowl and stir with a whisk. Thoroughly mix the plant milk, applesauce, brown sugar, oil, ground flaxseed, and vanilla extract in a medium bowl. Pour the wet mixture into the flour mixture and stir just until blended. Let stand for 5 minutes, while preheating the waffle iron according to the manufacturer's directions.

Spray both grids of the waffle iron generously with oil. Pour or ladle the batter into the center of the iron, covering no more than two-thirds of the iron's surface for the first waffle. Adjust the amount as needed for subsequent waffles. Bake each waffle for 3 to 5 minutes, or until it can be removed easily.

Heartfelt Banana-Spelt Waffles

Makes 3 to 4 (7 in. or 18 cm) round Belgian waffles

These feature the unique lightness and fluffiness of spelt, joined with natural banana-laden sweetness. When you bake them for someone, they'll know that you care. For an extra burst of banananess, pour some Banana-Maple-Nut Syrup (page 126) all over them.

> 2 1/4 cups (348 g) spelt flour
> 2 teaspoons baking powder
> 1/2 teaspoon salt
> 1 ripe medium banana (1/3 cup, 80 ml, or 90 g peeled and mashed)
> 2 cups (475 ml) soy milk or other plant milk
> 1/4 cup (60 ml) canola or other vegetable oil
> 2 tablespoons brown sugar
> 2 tablespoons ground flaxseed
> 1 teaspoon vanilla extract

Combine the flour, baking powder, and salt in a large bowl and stir with a whisk. Mash the banana in a medium bowl, and thoroughly mix with the plant milk, oil, brown sugar, ground flaxseed, and vanilla extract. Pour the wet mixture into the flour mixture and stir just until blended. Let stand for 2 to 3 minutes.

Stir the mixture another 5 to 10 strokes. Let it stand for 5 more minutes, while preheating the waffle iron according to the manufacturer's directions.

Spray both grids of the iron generously with oil. Pour or ladle the batter into the center of the iron, covering no more than two-thirds of the iron's surface for the first waffle. Adjust the amount as needed for subsequent waffles. Bake each waffle for 4 to 6 minutes, or until it can be removed easily.

Vegan Sourdough Waffles

Makes 4 (7 in. or 18 cm) round Belgian waffles.

Behold a treat for demanding vegan waffle lovers. These use natural sourdough fermentation, sugar provided by banana, and fat provided by coconut milk. Drizzle with maple syrup and top with a dollop of Coconut Whipped Cream (page 148).

Important: This recipe assumes you already maintain a sourdough starter. It requires night-before preparation.

> **1 cup (145 g) all-purpose flour**
> **1 cup (140 g) whole wheat flour**
> **1 1/2 cups (360 ml) water, divided**
> **1/2 cup (120 ml) sourdough starter (see note)**
> **1 teaspoon salt**
> **1 ripe medium banana (1/3 cup, 80 ml, or 90 g peeled and mashed)**
> **1/2 cup (120 ml) full-fat coconut milk**
> **1/2 teaspoon baking powder**
> **1/2 teaspoon baking soda**

Combine the all-purpose flour, whole wheat flour, 1 1/4 cups (300 ml) of the water, sourdough starter, and salt in a large non-metal bowl and stir until well blended. Cover loosely with plastic and allow to ferment at room temperature overnight, or 10 to 12 hours.

In the morning, mash the banana in a small bowl. Add the banana, coconut milk, remaining 1/4 cup (60 ml) water, baking powder, and baking soda to the mixture in the large bowl. Stir with a pair of chopsticks or the handle end of a spoon until most strands of the fermented portion are broken up into clumps smaller than your pinky finger and evenly distributed. Don't try to stir the batter until it's smooth, though. You want it somewhat lumpy, so the waffles don't end up tough.

Allow the batter to stand for 15 minutes. Preheat the waffle iron according to the manufacturer's directions, while the batter is standing.

Spray both grids of the waffle iron generously with oil. Pour or ladle the batter into the center of the iron, covering no more than two-thirds of the iron's surface for the first waffle. Adjust the amount as needed for subsequent waffles. Bake each waffle for 3 to 5 minutes, or until it can be removed easily.

Notes: This recipe was created with sourdough starter at roughly 100% hydration, unfed and stirred down before measuring.

For sweeter and slightly crispier waffles, add 2 tablespoons brown sugar or molasses when you mix in the banana and remaining ingredients.

If you're unfamiliar with sourdough baking and this recipe has piqued your curiosity, don't let phrases like "100% hydration" scare you away. That simply means that I used a starter containing roughly equal weights of water and flour (or about half as much water as flour when measuring both by volume).

Gluten-Free Naked Vegan Waffles (GF)

Makes 4 (7 in. or 18 cm) round Belgian waffles

This simple and easy recipe will satisfy a broad range of wafflicionados. Top these light and crispy treats with blueberries, mango, maple syrup, or pretty much any sweet or savory topping.

  1 3/4 cups (410 ml) soy milk or other plant milk
  1/4 cup (60 ml) canola or other vegetable oil
  1/4 cup (22 g) ground flaxseed
  1/4 cup (46 g) brown sugar
  1 1/2 cups plus 2 tablespoons (256 g) rice flour
  1/2 cup plus 2 tablespoons (80 g) tapioca flour
  2 teaspoons baking powder
  1 teaspoon baking soda
  1 teaspoon salt

Combine the plant milk, oil, ground flaxseed, and brown sugar in a medium bowl and mix thoroughly. Combine the rice flour, tapioca flour, baking powder, baking soda, and salt in a large bowl and stir with a whisk. Pour the liquid mixture into the flour mixture and stir until well blended and any large clumps are gone.

Let stand for 3 to 5 minutes, while preheating the waffle iron according to the manufacturer's directions.

Stir the batter another 5 to 10 strokes, to get rid of any remaining rice flour clumps. Spray both grids of the iron generously with oil—this is especially important for gluten-free recipes with flaxseed, even if your iron is "non-stick." Pour or ladle the batter into the center of the iron, covering no more than two-thirds of the iron's surface for the first waffle. Adjust the amount as needed for subsequent waffles. Bake each waffle for 3 to 5 minutes, or until it can be removed easily.

Mapley Waffles (GF)

Makes 4 (7 in. or 18 cm) round Belgian waffles

These are cousins of the Naked Vegan Waffles (page 41), plus baked-in maple flavor, minus the wheat. To increase the sweetness and texture, sprinkle with brown sugar and crushed walnuts.

> 1 3/4 cups (276 g) brown rice flour
> 1/2 cup (64 g) tapioca flour
> 2 teaspoons baking powder
> 1 teaspoon baking soda
> 1 teaspoon salt
> 1 1/2 teaspoons xanthan gum powder
> 2 cups (475 ml) soy milk or other plant milk
> 1/2 cup (120 ml) canola or other vegetable oil
> 1/2 cup (120 ml) maple syrup
> 1 1/2 teaspoons vanilla extract
> 1 teaspoon lemon juice or cider vinegar

Combine the brown rice flour, tapioca flour, baking powder, baking soda, salt, and xanthan gum powder in a large bowl and stir with a whisk. Thoroughly mix the plant milk, oil, maple syrup, vanilla extract, and lemon juice in a medium bowl. Pour the wet mixture into the flour mixture and stir until well blended and any large clumps are gone.

Let stand for 3 to 5 minutes, while preheating the waffle iron according to the manufacturer's directions.

Stir the batter another 5 to 10 strokes, to get rid of any remaining rice flour clumps. Spray both grids generously with oil. Pour or ladle the batter into the center of the iron, covering no more than two-thirds of the iron's surface for the first waffle. Adjust the amount as needed for subsequent waffles. Bake each waffle for 3 to 5 minutes, or until it can be removed easily.

Sinfully Cinnamon Mapley Waffles: Add 1 1/2 teaspoons ground cinnamon to the flour mixture.

Nice Rice-Teff Waffles (GF)

Makes 4 (7 in. or 18 cm) round Belgian waffles

These are just a little crispier and slightly sweeter than the Mapley Waffles (page 50). The teff flour takes it to a wholenutha level. For a special treat or a decadent breakfast, sandwich a few scoops of Mango-Vanilla Ice Cream (page 137) between two waffle quarters.

1 1/4 cups (197 g) brown rice flour
1/2 cup (64 g) tapioca flour
1/2 cup (70 g) teff flour (different from whole grain teff)
2 teaspoons baking powder
1 teaspoon baking soda
1 1/4 teaspoons salt
1 teaspoon xanthan gum powder
1 3/4 cups plus 2 tablespoons (440 ml) soy milk or other plant milk
1/4 cup plus 2 tablespoons (69 g) brown sugar
1/4 cup plus 2 tablespoons (90 ml) canola or other vegetable oil
1/4 cup (60 ml) maple syrup
1 1/2 teaspoons vanilla extract

Combine the brown rice flour, tapioca flour, teff flour, baking powder, baking soda, salt, and xanthan gum powder in a large bowl and stir with a whisk. Thoroughly mix the plant milk, brown sugar, oil, maple syrup, and vanilla extract in a medium bowl. Pour the wet mixture into the flour mixture and stir until well blended and any large clumps are gone.

Let stand for 3 to 5 minutes, while preheating the waffle iron according to the manufacturer's directions.

Stir the batter another 5 to 10 strokes, to get rid of any remaining rice flour clumps. Spray both grids of the iron generously with oil. Pour or ladle the batter into the center of the iron, covering no more than two-thirds of the iron's surface for the first waffle. Adjust the amount as needed for subsequent waffles. Bake each waffle for 3 to 5 minutes, or until it can be removed easily.

Textured Rice Waffles (GF)

Makes 4 (7 in. or 18 cm) round Belgian waffles

These siblings of the Nice Rice-Teff Waffles (page 51) replace the teff flour with the increased texture of whole grain teff and utilize ground flaxseed in lieu of xanthan gum. Serve up with a topping of sliced banana and Maple Syrup Supreme (page 128) or heat some peanut butter and pour it on.

2 cups (475 ml) soy milk or other plant milk
1/4 cup plus 2 tablespoons (69 g) brown sugar
1/4 cup plus 2 tablespoons (90 ml) canola or other vegetable oil
1/4 cup (22 g) ground flaxseed
1/4 cup (60 ml) maple syrup
1 1/2 teaspoons vanilla extract
1 1/2 cups (237 g) brown rice flour
1/2 cup (64 g) tapioca flour
1/4 cup (52 g) whole grain teff (different from teff flour)
2 teaspoons baking powder
1 teaspoon baking soda
1 1/4 teaspoons salt

Thoroughly mix the plant milk, brown sugar, oil, flaxseed, maple syrup, and vanilla extract in a medium bowl. Combine the brown rice flour, tapioca flour, whole grain teff, baking powder, baking soda, and salt in a large bowl and stir with a whisk. Pour the wet mixture into the flour mixture and stir until well blended and any large clumps are gone.

Let stand for 3 to 5 minutes, while preheating the waffle iron according to the manufacturer's directions.

Stir the batter another 5 to 10 strokes, to get rid of any remaining rice flour clumps. Spray both grids of the iron generously with oil—this is especially important for gluten-free recipes with flaxseed, even if your iron is "non-stick." Pour or ladle the batter into the center of the iron, covering no more than two-thirds of the iron's surface for the first waffle. Adjust the amount as needed for subsequent waffles. Bake each waffle for 3 to 5 minutes, or until it can be removed easily.

Yeasted Buckwheat Waffles (GF)

Makes 4 (7 in. or 18 cm) round Belgian waffles

With a wholesome flavor and texture, these are also great syrup sponges. Because the batter needs time to rise, begin at least 3 hours in advance of baking or 1 1/2 hours in advance if you are using quick-rise yeast. Top with raspberries, blueberries, and a generous drizzling of Maple Syrup Supreme (page 128).

> 1 1/4 teaspoons active dry yeast
> 2 1/4 cups (535 ml) warm water, divided
>   (see "Yeasted Waffle Tips," page 23)
> 1 1/4 cups (200 g) brown rice flour
> 1 cup (150 g) buckwheat flour
> 1 teaspoon salt
> 3 tablespoons canola or other vegetable oil
> 2 tablespoons ground flaxseed
> 2 tablespoons molasses
> 1 1/4 teaspoons baking powder

Dissolve the yeast in 2 cups (475 ml) of warm water in a large non-metal bowl. Let stand for 5 minutes. Stir in the rice flour, buckwheat flour, and salt until well blended. Cover the bowl and place it in a warm location so the flour mixture can rise—for at least 3 hours, or 1 1/2 hours if using quick-rise yeast. (See "Yeasted Waffle Tips," page 23). Because this is a gluten-free mixture, it may expand only slightly, but the process will still add some flavor and texture.

After the flour mixture has risen, combine 1/4 cup (60 ml) warm water, oil, ground flaxseed, molasses, and baking powder in a small bowl. Mix thoroughly, breaking up any clumps of baking powder. Immediately pour into the flour mixture and stir until well blended. Let stand for 15 minutes, while preheating the waffle iron according to the manufacturer's directions.

Spray both grids of the waffle iron generously with oil—this is especially important for gluten-free recipes with flaxseed, even with "non-stick" irons. Pour or ladle batter into the center of the iron, covering no more than two-thirds of the iron's surface for the first waffle. Adjust the amount as needed for subsequent waffles. Bake each waffle for 3 to 5 minutes, or until it can be removed easily.

Buckwheat-Molasses Waffles (GF)

Makes 4 (7 in. or 18 cm) round Belgian waffles

These are slightly sweeter than the Yeasted Buckwheat Waffles (page 53), with half the molasses of the Molasses-Tastic Waffles (page 88). Round out the picture with fresh blackberries and a dollop of vegan vanilla ice cream.

> 1 cup (150 g) buckwheat flour
> 1 cup (158 g) brown rice flour
> 1/2 cup (64 g) tapioca flour
> 2 teaspoons baking powder
> 1 teaspoon baking soda
> 1 teaspoon salt
> 2 teaspoons xanthan gum powder
> 2 1/2 cups (590 ml) soy milk or other plant milk
> 1/4 cup (60 ml) canola or other vegetable oil
> 2 tablespoons sugar
> 2 tablespoons molasses

Combine the buckwheat flour, rice flour, tapioca flour, baking powder, baking soda, salt, and xanthan gum powder in a large bowl and stir with a whisk. Thoroughly mix the plant milk, oil, sugar, and molasses in a medium bowl. Pour the wet mixture into the flour mixture and stir until well blended and any large clumps are gone. Let stand for 3 to 5 minutes, while preheating the waffle iron according to the manufacturer's directions.

Stir the batter another 5 to 10 strokes, to get rid of any remaining rice flour clumps. Spray both grids of the waffle iron generously with oil. Pour or ladle the batter into the center of the iron, covering no more than two-thirds of the iron's surface for the first waffle. Adjust the amount as needed for subsequent waffles. Bake each waffle for 4 to 5 minutes, or until it can be removed easily.

Crunchy Steel City Waffles (GF)

Makes 4 (7 in. or 18 cm) round Belgian waffles

These champions feature bits of chewy steel-cut oats and a hint of molasses to satisfy your tough side. Bump them up a notch with the Creamy Spiced Apple Pie Sauce (page 134).

  1 3/4 cups (276 g) brown rice flour
  1/2 cup (64 g) tapioca flour
  1/4 cup (44 g) steel-cut oats
  2 teaspoons baking powder
  1 teaspoon baking soda
  3/4 teaspoon salt
  1 teaspoon xanthan gum powder
  1 1/2 cups (350 ml) soy milk or other plant milk
  1/2 cup (120 ml) smooth applesauce
  1/4 cup (60 ml) canola or other vegetable oil
  1/4 cup (60 ml) maple syrup
  2 tablespoons molasses
  1 teaspoon vanilla extract

Combine the brown rice flour, tapioca flour, oats, baking powder, baking soda, salt, and xanthan gum powder in a large bowl and stir with a whisk. Thoroughly mix the plant milk, applesauce, oil, maple syrup, molasses, and vanilla extract in a medium bowl. Pour the wet mixture into the flour mixture and stir until well blended and any large clumps are gone. Let stand for 3 to 5 minutes, while preheating the waffle iron according to the manufacturer's directions.

Stir the batter another 5 to 10 strokes, to get rid of any remaining rice flour clumps. Spray both grids of the waffle iron generously with oil. Pour or ladle the batter into the center of the iron, covering no more than two-thirds of the iron's surface for the first waffle. Adjust the amount as needed for subsequent waffles. Bake each waffle for 3 to 5 minutes, or until it can be removed easily.

Crispy Cornbuck Waffles (GF)

Makes 4 (7 in. or 18 cm) round Belgian waffles

A waffle with a name that sounds like a cartoon hero, Crispy Cornbuck is a powerful culinary force. He just might save your day. Partner with the savory heartiness of Southwestern Beans and Greens (page 156), or the country-style sweetness of Maple Syrup Supreme (page 128).

2 cups plus 2 tablespoons (505 ml) soy milk or other plant milk
1/4 cup (60 ml) canola or other vegetable oil
1/4 cup (22 g) ground flaxseed
1/4 cup (60 ml) maple syrup
2 tablespoons molasses
2/3 cup (104 g) brown rice flour
2/3 cup (89 g) buckwheat flour
2/3 cup (110 g) cornmeal
1/2 cup (64 g) tapioca flour
2 teaspoons baking powder
1 teaspoon baking soda
1 teaspoon salt

Thoroughly mix the plant milk, oil, ground flaxseed, maple syrup, and molasses in a medium bowl. Combine the brown rice flour, buckwheat flour, cornmeal, tapioca flour, baking powder, baking soda, and salt in a large bowl and stir with a whisk. Pour the wet mixture into the flour mixture and stir until well blended and any large clumps are gone. Let stand for 3 to 5 minutes, while preheating the waffle iron according to the manufacturer's directions.

Stir the batter another 5 to 10 strokes, to get rid of any remaining rice flour clumps. Spray both grids of the iron generously with oil—this is especially important for gluten-free recipes with flaxseed, even if your iron is "non-stick." Pour or ladle the batter into the center of the iron, covering no more than two-thirds of the iron's surface for the first waffle. Adjust the amount as needed for subsequent waffles. Bake each waffle for 3 to 5 minutes, or until it can be removed easily.

Zero Excuse Rice-Coconut Waffles (GF)

Makes 5 (7 in. or 18 cm) round Belgian waffles.

While all vegan waffles are dairy-free, egg-free, and cholesterol-free, these are also gluten-free and oil-free. They leave few excuses for not eating a waffle. With a slightly crispy exterior and a molasses-enriched flavor, they go well with a range of toppings. To keep it simple, try warm applesauce and cinnamon.

    1 3/4 cups (410 ml) full-fat coconut milk
    1 3/4 cups (410 ml) warm water
    1/4 cup (22 g) ground flaxseed
    3 tablespoons molasses
    2 cups (316 g) brown rice flour
    1/2 cup (64 g) tapioca flour
    2 teaspoons baking powder
    1 teaspoon baking soda
    1 teaspoon salt

Thoroughly mix the coconut milk, warm water, ground flaxseed, and molasses in a medium bowl. Combine the rice flour, tapioca flour, baking powder, baking soda, and salt in a large bowl and stir with a whisk. Pour the wet ingredients into the dry and mix until the batter is only slightly lumpy, with lumps smaller than peas.

While allowing the batter to stand for 3 to 5 minutes, preheat the waffle iron according to the manufacturer's directions.

Stir the batter another 5 to 10 strokes, breaking up any clumps of rice flour that haven't absorbed moisture. Spray both grids of the iron generously with oil—this is especially important for gluten-free recipes with flaxseed, even if your iron is "non-stick." Pour or ladle the batter into the center of the iron, covering no more than two-thirds of the iron's surface for the first waffle. Adjust the amount as needed for subsequent waffles. Bake each waffle for 4 to 5 minutes, or until it can be removed easily.

Simple Yeasted Rice Waffles (GF)

Makes 4 (7 in. or 18 cm) round Belgian waffles.

These delectably light, chewy, slightly crispy treats exhibit the magic of fermented rice flour. Because the batter needs time to ferment, begin at least 3 hours in advance of baking or 1 1/2 hours in advance if you are using quick-rise yeast. Top with a classic blend of maple syrup, Coconut Whipped Cream (page 148), and a flurry of cinnamon.

> 1 1/4 teaspoons active dry yeast
> 1 3/4 cups (410 ml) warm water (see "Yeasted Waffle Tips," page 23)
> 1 3/4 cups plus 2 tablespoons (296 g) brown rice flour
> 1/2 cup plus 2 tablespoons (80 g) tapioca flour
> 1 1/4 teaspoons salt
> 1/4 cup (60 ml) canola or other vegetable oil
> 1/4 cup (22 g) ground flaxseed
> 1/4 cup (60 ml) maple syrup
> 1 1/2 teaspoons baking powder

Dissolve the yeast in the water in a large non-metal bowl. Let stand for 5 minutes. Stir in the rice flour, tapioca flour, and salt until well blended. Cover the bowl and place it in a warm location so the flour mixture can ferment—for at least 3 hours, or 1 1/2 hours if using quick-rise yeast (see "Yeasted Waffle Tips," page 23). Because this is a gluten-free mixture, it may expand only slightly, but the process will add flavor and texture.

After the flour mixture has fermented, combine the oil, ground flaxseed, maple syrup, and baking powder in a small bowl. Mix thoroughly, breaking up any clumps of baking powder. Pour into the fermented flour mixture and stir until well blended. Let stand for 15 minutes, while preheating the waffle iron according to the manufacturer's directions.

Spray both grids of the waffle iron generously with oil—this is especially important for gluten-free recipes with flaxseed, even if your iron is "non-stick." Pour or ladle the batter into the center of the iron, covering no more than two-thirds of the iron's surface for the first waffle. Adjust the amount as needed for subsequent waffles. Bake each waffle for 3 to 5 minutes, or until it can be removed easily.

Dave's Fave Waffle Party Waffles (GF)

Makes 4 (7 in. or 18 cm) round Belgian waffles.

I've baked these fluffy, crispy treats for several waffle parties, and they've received much praise. They are a hybrid of several other recipes, including the Gluten-Free Naked Vegan Waffles (page 49). Because the baked-in molasses and maple flavor is subtle, they go well with a range of toppings, which is important for a waffle party.

> 1 1/4 cups (300 ml) warm water
> 3/4 cup (180 ml) full-fat coconut milk
> 1/4 cup (22 g) ground flaxseed
> 1/4 cup (60 ml) maple syrup (see note)
> 3 tablespoons canola or other vegetable oil
> 1 tablespoon molasses
> 1 1/2 cups (237 g) brown rice flour
> 1/2 cup (64 g) tapioca flour
> 1/4 cup (35 g) teff flour (different from whole grain teff; see note)
> 2 teaspoons baking powder
> 1 teaspoon baking soda
> 1 teaspoon salt

Combine the warm water, coconut milk, ground flaxseed, maple syrup, oil, and molasses in a medium bowl and mix thoroughly. Combine the rice flour, tapioca flour, teff flour, baking powder, baking soda, and salt in a large bowl and stir with a whisk. Pour the liquid mixture into the flour mixture and stir until well blended and any large clumps are gone.

Let stand for 3 to 5 minutes, while preheating the waffle iron according to the manufacturer's directions.

Stir the batter another 5 to 10 strokes, to get rid of any remaining rice flour clumps. Spray both grids of the iron generously with oil—this is especially important for gluten-free recipes with flaxseed, even if your iron is "non-stick." Pour or ladle the batter into the center of the iron, covering no more than two-thirds of the iron's surface for the first waffle. Adjust the amount as needed for subsequent waffles. Bake each waffle for 3 to 5 minutes, or until it can be removed easily.

Notes: If you prefer to use brown sugar instead of maple syrup, use 1/4 cup plus 1 tablespoon (58 g) brown sugar and add 1 tablespoon water to the recipe.

If you don't have teff flour, add 3 tablespoons brown rice flour and 1 tablespoon tapioca flour to the recipe.

Flavory-Sweet Waffles

While the Neutral Waffles section contains some relatively sweet recipes, the waffles in this section blend sweetness with rich flavor combinations. These range from ginger-lemon-chocolate (page 66) to mango-chili (page 76). There's no reason to limit them to dessert, as they can be enjoyed at any time. For example, the Espresso-Key Lime Waffles (page 75) or the Yeast-Raised Cinnamon-Raisin Waffles (page 64) are well suited for breakfast or brunch.

Original Cinnamon-Raisin Waffles

Makes 5 (7 in. or 18 cm) round Belgian waffles

This classic flavor combination is great for any occasion, and this version can be prepared on shorter notice than the Yeast-Raised Cinnamon-Raisin Waffles (page 64). For a level of sweetness approximating a cinnamon roll, drizzle generously with Cinnamon Cream Cheese (page 132). Finely chopped walnuts add a flavorful topping twist.

> 1 1/4 cups (181 g) all-purpose flour
> 1 cup (140 g) whole wheat flour
> 1/2 cup (56 g) rolled oats
> 2 teaspoons baking powder
> 1 teaspoon baking soda
> 1 1/2 teaspoons salt
> 1 tablespoon ground cinnamon
> 2 cups (475 ml) soy milk or other plant milk
> 1/2 cup (92 g) brown sugar
> 1/2 cup (120 ml) canola or other vegetable oil
> 1/4 cup (60 ml) maple syrup
> 1 1/2 teaspoons vanilla extract
> 1/2 cup (80 g) raisins

Combine the all-purpose flour, whole wheat flour, oats, baking powder, baking soda, salt, and cinnamon in a large bowl and stir with a whisk. Thoroughly mix the plant milk, brown sugar, oil, maple syrup, and vanilla extract in a medium bowl. Pour the wet mixture into the flour mixture and stir just until blended. Fold in the raisins.

Preheat the waffle iron according to the manufacturer's directions. Spray both grids with oil. Pour or ladle the batter into the center of the iron, covering no more than two-thirds of the iron's surface for the first waffle. Adjust the amount as needed for subsequent waffles. Bake each waffle for 3 to 4 minutes, or until it can be removed easily.

Yeast-Raised Cinnamon-Raisin Waffles

Makes 5 (7 in. or 18 cm) round Belgian waffles

These deliver the same delicious flavor combination as the Original Cinnamon-Raisin Waffles (page 63), with a chewier, bread-like texture. They're a great brunch alternative to French toast, and they make a great dessert when covered with Cinnamon Cream Cheese (page 132). Because the batter needs time to rise, begin at least 3 hours in advance of baking or 1 1/2 hours in advance if you are using quick-rise yeast.

> 1 1/4 teaspoons active dry yeast
> 1 1/2 cups (350 ml) warm water (see "Yeasted Waffle Tips," page 23)
> 1 cup (145 g) all-purpose flour
> 3/4 cup (105 g) whole wheat flour
> 3/4 cup (84 g) rolled oats
> 1/4 cup (60 ml) maple syrup
> 1 1/2 teaspoons salt
> 1/2 cup (120 ml) soy milk or other plant milk
> 1/2 cup (92 g) brown sugar
> 1/4 cup plus 2 tablespoons (90 ml) canola or other vegetable oil
> 2 tablespoons cider vinegar
> 1 tablespoon ground cinnamon
> 1 1/2 teaspoons vanilla extract
> 3/4 teaspoon baking soda
> 1/2 teaspoon baking powder
> 1/2 cup (80 g) raisins

Dissolve the yeast in the water in a large non-metal bowl. Let stand for 5 minutes. Stir in the all-purpose flour, whole wheat flour, oats, syrup, and salt until well blended. Cover the bowl and place it in a warm location until the flour mixture has almost doubled (see "Yeasted Waffle Tips," page 23).

After the flour mixture has risen, combine the plant milk, brown sugar, oil, vinegar, cinnamon, vanilla extract, baking soda, and baking powder in a small bowl. Mix thoroughly, breaking up any clumps of baking soda or baking powder. Pour into the raised flour mixture and stir until well blended. Fold in the raisins.

Let stand for 15 minutes, while preheating the waffle iron according to the manufacturer's directions.

Spray both grids of the waffle iron with oil. Pour or ladle the batter into the center of the iron, covering no more than two-thirds of the iron's surface for the first waffle. Adjust the amount as needed for subsequent waffles. Bake each waffle for 3 to 4 minutes, or until it can be removed easily.

Generously Ginger-Lemon-Chocolate Waffles

Makes 4 to 5 (7 in. or 18 cm) round Belgian waffles

If you're a gingerchocolafanatic, these will hit the spot. They incorporate both fresh and candied ginger for enhanced warmth. Top with vegan ice cream and Dark Chocolate Syrup (page 125), Crazeee Carob Syrup (page 126), or Lemon-Ginger Drizzle (page 130).

1/4 cup (42 g) semisweet chocolate or carob chips, finely chopped
1/4 cup (42 g) finely chopped candied ginger
1 tablespoon plus 1 teaspoon fresh grated ginger root
1 1/2 cups (218 g) all-purpose flour
1 cup (140 g) whole wheat flour
2 teaspoons baking powder
1 teaspoon baking soda
1 teaspoon salt
1 1/2 cups (350 ml) soy milk or other plant milk
1 cup (200 g) sugar
1/4 cup plus 2 tablespoons (90 ml) canola or other vegetable oil
1/4 cup (60 ml) lemon juice
1 teaspoon vanilla extract

Chop the chocolate chips and candied ginger, grate the ginger root, and set aside. Combine the all-purpose flour, whole wheat flour, baking powder, baking soda, and salt in a large bowl and stir with a whisk. Thoroughly mix the fresh grated ginger root, plant milk, sugar, oil, lemon juice, and vanilla extract in a medium bowl. Pour the wet mixture into the flour mixture and stir just until blended. Fold in the chocolate chips and candied ginger.

Preheat the waffle iron according to the manufacturer's directions. Spray both grids with oil. Pour or ladle the batter into the center of the iron, covering no more than two-thirds of the iron's surface for the first waffle. Adjust the amount as needed for subsequent waffles. Bake each waffle for 3 to 4 minutes, or until it can be removed easily.

Dark Chocolate Cake Waffles

Makes 5 (7 in. or 18 cm) round Belgian waffles

Are you craving cake but don't feel like waiting for it to bake in the oven? Enjoy these delectable desserts with Cocoa or Carob Agave Nectar (page 127), Coco Kah-banana Syrup (page 129), or Creamy Maple-Chai Dream Sauce (page 133). Or, top with fresh strawberries or raspberries for a bit of tartness and color.

> 1 1/2 cups (218 g) all-purpose flour
> 1/2 cup (70 g) whole wheat flour
> 1/2 cup (44 g) cocoa powder
> 1 1/2 teaspoons baking powder
> 1 teaspoon baking soda
> 1 teaspoon salt
> 2 1/3 cups (555 ml) soy milk or other plant milk
> 3/4 cup (180 ml) canola or other vegetable oil
> 1/2 cup plus 2 tablespoons (115 g) brown sugar
> 1 1/2 teaspoons vanilla extract

Combine the all-purpose flour, whole wheat flour, cocoa powder, baking powder, baking soda, and salt in a large bowl and stir with a whisk. Break up any clumps of cocoa. Thoroughly mix the plant milk, oil, brown sugar, and vanilla extract in a medium bowl. Pour the wet mixture into the flour mixture and stir just until blended. If necessary, use a spoon or spatula to break up any cocoa clumps and push the cocoa down into the batter.

Preheat the waffle iron according to the manufacturer's directions. Spray both grids with oil. Pour or ladle the batter into the center of the iron, covering no more than two-thirds of the iron's surface for the first waffle. Adjust the amount as needed for subsequent waffles. Bake each waffle for 2 to 4 minutes, or until it is still moist but can be removed easily.

Hot Chocolate-Molasses Waffles

Makes 5 to 6 (7 in. or 18 cm) round Belgian waffles

Dark, sweet chocolate and spice warm up the taste buds. These moist, cakelike treats can follow dinner, or you can serve them to that special someone for a breakfast or brunch in bed. For added flare, garnish with chocolate chips and a dusting of cinnamon.

1 1/2 cups (218 g) all-purpose flour
1/2 cup (70 g) whole wheat flour
1/2 cup (44 g) cocoa powder
1 1/2 teaspoons baking powder
1 teaspoon baking soda
1 teaspoon salt
1 1/2 teaspoons chili powder
1/8 teaspoon ground cayenne
2 1/4 cups (530 ml) soy milk or other plant milk
3/4 cup (180 ml) canola or other vegetable oil
1/2 cup (100 g) sugar
1/4 cup (60 ml) molasses
1 teaspoon vanilla extract

Combine the all-purpose flour, whole wheat flour, cocoa powder, baking powder, baking soda, salt, chili powder, and cayenne in a large bowl and stir with a whisk. Break up any clumps of cocoa. Thoroughly mix the plant milk, oil, sugar, molasses, and vanilla extract in a small bowl. Pour the wet mixture into the flour mixture and stir just until blended. If necessary, use a spoon or spatula to break up any cocoa clumps and push the cocoa down into the batter.

Preheat the waffle iron according to the manufacturer's directions. Spray both grids with oil. Pour or ladle the batter into the center of the iron, covering no more than two-thirds of the iron's surface for the first waffle. Adjust the amount as needed for subsequent waffles. Bake each waffle for 3 to 4 minutes, or until it is still moist but can be removed easily.

PBMax (Peanut Butter to the Max) Waffles

Makes 4 (7 in. or 18 cm) round Belgian waffles

What is the maximum amount of peanut butter a batter can contain and still become a waffle? These waffles appear to come close. Garnish with Cocoa or Carob Agave Nectar (page 127), Dark Chocolate Syrup (page 125), jelly or jam, or sliced bananas.

1/2 cup (73 g) all-purpose flour
1/2 cup (70 g) whole wheat flour
1/4 cup (28 g) rolled oats
1 teaspoon baking powder
3/4 teaspoon baking soda
3/4 teaspoon salt
1/2 teaspoon xanthan gum powder
1 1/4 cups (300 ml) soy milk or other plant milk
3/4 cup (192 g) smooth peanut butter (see note)
1/2 cup (120 ml) smooth applesauce
1/4 cup (46 g) brown sugar
3 tablespoons canola or other vegetable oil
1 teaspoon vanilla extract

Combine the all-purpose flour, whole wheat flour, oats, baking powder, baking soda, salt, and xanthan gum powder in a large bowl and stir with a whisk. Thoroughly mix the plant milk, peanut butter, applesauce, brown sugar, oil, and vanilla extract in a small bowl. Pour the wet mixture into the flour mixture and stir just until blended. Let stand for 3 to 4 minutes, while preheating the waffle iron according to the manufacturer's directions.

Spray both grids of the waffle iron with oil. Pour or ladle the batter into the center of the iron, covering no more than two-thirds of the iron's surface for the first waffle. Adjust the amount as needed for subsequent waffles. Bake each waffle for 3 to 4 minutes, or until it can be removed easily.

Note: If you're using peanut butter that has been refrigerated, warming it in the microwave may make it easier to mix into the batter.

Cider-Pecan Waffles

Makes 4 (7 in. or 18 cm) round Belgian waffles

These are reminiscent of the sugary, warm cider donuts that country orchards and grocers sell in the late summer and fall. Complete with melted vegan butter and a sprinkling of sugar, Creamy Spiced Apple Pie Sauce (page 134), or just a little hot maple syrup.

1/3 cup (40 g) finely chopped raw pecans
1 cup (145 g) all-purpose flour
1 cup (140 g) whole wheat flour
2 teaspoons baking powder
1 teaspoon baking soda
1 teaspoon salt
1/2 teaspoon xanthan gum powder
1/2 teaspoon ground cinnamon
1/4 teaspoon ground or grated nutmeg
1 1/2 cups (350 ml) apple cider
1/2 cup plus 2 tablespoons (150 ml) soy milk or other plant milk
3/4 cup (150 g) sugar
1/2 cup (120 ml) canola or other vegetable oil
1 teaspoon vanilla extract

Chop the pecans and set aside. Combine the all-purpose flour, whole wheat flour, baking powder, baking soda, salt, xanthan gum powder, cinnamon, and nutmeg in a large bowl and stir with a whisk. Thoroughly mix the apple cider, plant milk, sugar, oil, and vanilla extract in a medium bowl. Pour the wet mixture into the flour mixture and stir just until blended. Fold in the chopped pecans.

Preheat the waffle iron according to the manufacturer's directions. Spray both grids with oil. Pour or ladle the batter into the center of the iron, covering no more than two-thirds of the iron's surface for the first waffle. Adjust the amount as needed for subsequent waffles. Bake each waffle for 4 to 5 minutes, or until it can be removed easily.

Sinful Cheesecakey Waffles

Makes 3 (7 in. or 18 cm) round Belgian waffles

With a light lemony flavor somewhere between a vegan cheese danish and a cheesecake, these have a dense, chewy texture. These are delicious with Amazing Amaretto Sauce (page 135), Lemon-Ginger Drizzle (page 130), strawberries, or blueberries.

> 1 cup plus 2 tablespoons (163 g) all-purpose flour
> 1 1/4 teaspoons baking powder
> 1/2 teaspoon baking soda
> 3/4 teaspoon salt
> 1 1/2 teaspoons ground cinnamon
> 1 container (8 oz./227 g) plain non-hydrogenated vegan cream cheese
> 1/2 cup (120 ml) soy milk or other plant milk
> 1/2 cup (100 g) sugar
> 3 tablespoons canola or other vegetable oil
> 1/4 cup (60 ml) lemon juice
> 2 teaspoons vanilla extract

Combine the flour, baking powder, baking soda, salt, and cinnamon in a large bowl and stir with a whisk. Microwave the vegan cream cheese just until softened in a medium bowl. (This probably won't take more than 30 to 45 seconds.) Thoroughly mix the plant milk, sugar, oil, lemon juice, and vanilla extract with the vegan cream cheese. Pour the wet mixture into the flour mixture and stir just until blended.

Preheat the waffle iron according to the manufacturer's directions. Spray both grids with oil. Pour or ladle the batter into the center of the iron, covering no more than two-thirds of the iron's surface for the first waffle. Adjust the amount as needed for subsequent waffles. Bake each waffle for 4 to 6 minutes, or until it can be removed easily.

Chocolate-Raspberry Cheesecakey Waffles

Makes 3 (7 in. or 18 cm) round Belgian waffles

Blending deep chocolate with tangy sweetness, these decadent desserts dance on the tongue. For an exceptional treat, top with a large dollop of Raspberry-Avocado Cream (page 126).

1/2 cup (70 g) raspberries, chopped into quarters
1 cup plus 2 tablespoons (163 g) all-purpose flour
1/4 cup (22 g) cocoa powder
1 1/4 teaspoons baking powder
1/2 teaspoon baking soda
3/4 teaspoon salt
1 container (8 oz./227 g) plain non-hydrogenated vegan cream cheese
1/2 cup plus 2 tablespoons (150 ml) soy milk or other plant milk
1/2 cup (100 g) sugar
1/4 cup (60 ml) canola or other vegetable oil
2 tablespoons lime juice
2 teaspoons vanilla extract

Chop the raspberries and set aside. Combine the flour, cocoa powder, baking powder, baking soda, and salt in a large bowl and stir with a whisk. Microwave the vegan cream cheese just until softened in a medium bowl. (This probably won't take more than 30 to 45 seconds.) Thoroughly mix the plant milk, sugar, oil, lime juice, and vanilla extract with the vegan cream cheese. Pour the wet mixture into the flour mixture and stir just until blended. Fold in the raspberries.

Preheat the waffle iron according to the manufacturer's directions. Spray both grids with oil. Pour or ladle the batter into the center of the iron, covering no more than two-thirds of the iron's surface for the first waffle. Adjust the amount as needed for subsequent waffles. Bake each waffle for 4 to 6 minutes, or until it can be removed easily.

Chai Spice Waffles

Makes 3 (7 in. or 18 cm) round Belgian waffles

Chai-ching! Cash in with these high-value waffles, melding warm spices, a soothing aroma, and a dense and chewy texture. Enhance with Dark Chocolate Syrup (page 125), or top with Creamy Maple-Chai Dream Sauce (page 133) for a super chai charge.

1 cup plus 3 tablespoons (172 g) all-purpose flour
1 1/4 teaspoons baking powder
1/2 teaspoon baking soda
3/4 teaspoon salt
2 teaspoons ground cinnamon
2 teaspoons ground ginger
3/4 teaspoon allspice
3/4 teaspoon ground clove
3/4 teaspoon ground or grated nutmeg
1/4 teaspoon ground cardamom (optional)
1 container (8 oz./227 g) plain non-hydrogenated vegan cream cheese
3/4 cup (180 ml) soy milk or other plant milk
3/4 cup (150 g) sugar
3 tablespoons canola or other vegetable oil
1 tablespoon cider vinegar or lemon juice
2 teaspoons vanilla extract

Combine the flour, baking powder, baking soda, salt, cinnamon, ginger, allspice, clove, nutmeg, and cardamom in a large bowl and stir with a whisk. Microwave the vegan cream cheese just until softened in a medium bowl. (This probably won't take more than 30 to 45 seconds.) Thoroughly mix the plant milk, sugar, oil, vinegar, and vanilla extract with the vegan cream cheese. Pour the wet mixture into the flour mixture and stir just until blended.

Preheat the waffle iron according to the manufacturer's directions. Spray both grids with oil. Pour or ladle the batter into the center of the iron, covering no more than two-thirds of the iron's surface for the first waffle. Adjust the amount as needed for subsequent waffles. Bake each waffle for 4 to 5 minutes, or until it can be removed easily.

Almond-Amaranth Waffles

Makes 4 to 5 (7 in. or 18 cm) round Belgian waffles

These treats blend moderate sweetness with salty, toasted nuttiness. For a more pronounced and dessert-like flavor, drizzle with Amazing Amaretto Sauce (page 135) alongside the cherry halves.

> 1/2 cup (56 g) raw almonds, finely chopped
> 1/4 cup plus 2 tablespoons (90 ml) canola or other vegetable oil, divided
> 1 1/2 teaspoons salt, divided
> 1 1/4 cups (181 g) all-purpose flour
> 1 cup (140 g) amaranth flour
> 2 teaspoons baking powder
> 1 teaspoon baking soda
> 2 1/4 cups (530 ml) almond milk or other plant milk
> 1/2 cup (100 g) sugar
> 1/4 cup (60 ml) plain or vanilla dairy-free yogurt
> 2 tablespoons ground flaxseed
> 1 1/2 teaspoons almond extract
> 1 1/2 teaspoons vanilla extract
> 1/3 cup (60 g) drained/halved Maraschino cherries (optional topping)

Chop the almonds. Place them in a medium frying pan with 2 tablespoons of the oil and 1/4 teaspoon of the salt. Sauté over medium heat 4 to 5 minutes or until slightly brown and set aside. Combine the remaining 1 1/4 teaspoons of salt, all-purpose flour, amaranth flour, baking powder, and baking soda in a large bowl and stir with a whisk. Thoroughly mix the remaining 1/4 cup (60 ml) of oil, plant milk, sugar, dairy-free yogurt, flaxseed, almond extract, and vanilla extract in a medium bowl. Pour the wet mixture into the flour mixture and stir just until blended. Fold in the almonds.

Preheat the waffle iron according to the manufacturer's directions. Spray both grids with oil. Pour or ladle the batter into the center of the iron, covering no more than two-thirds of the iron's surface for the first waffle. Adjust the amount as needed for subsequent waffles. Bake each waffle for 3 to 5 minutes, or until it can be removed easily. Top with the cherry halves.

Espresso-Key Lime Waffles

Makes 4 (7 in. or 18 cm) round Belgian waffles

Each of these provides a cup of perk-you-up with a sweet citrus twist. Top with additional granola, Espresso-Maple-Walnut Syrup (page 128), or Coco Kahbanana Syrup (page 129).

1 1/4 cups (181 g) all-purpose flour
1 cup (140 g) whole wheat flour
2 teaspoons baking powder
1 teaspoon baking soda
1 teaspoon salt
1 teaspoon xanthan gum powder
3/4 cup (180 ml) hot water
2 tablespoons instant espresso granules
1 cup (240 ml) soy milk or other plant milk
1 cup (200 g) sugar
1/2 cup plus 2 tablespoons (150 ml) canola or other vegetable oil
1/4 cup (60 ml) fresh key lime juice (about 6 key limes, see note)
1 teaspoon vanilla extract
3/4 cup (roughly 75 g) granola, maple-flavored or other

Combine the all-purpose flour, whole wheat flour, baking powder, baking soda, salt, and xanthan gum powder in a large bowl and stir with a whisk. Dissolve the espresso granules in the hot water in a medium bowl. The hottest water from the tap should work. Thoroughly mix the plant milk, sugar, oil, key lime juice, and vanilla extract with the dissolved coffee. Pour the wet mixture into the flour mixture and stir just until blended. Fold in the granola.

Preheat the waffle iron according to the manufacturer's directions. Spray both grids with oil. Pour or ladle the batter into the center of the iron, covering no more than two-thirds of the iron's surface for the first waffle. Adjust the amount as needed for subsequent waffles. Bake each waffle for 3 to 4 minutes, or until it can be removed easily.

Note: You may substitute 2 tablespoons lemon juice plus 2 tablespoons regular lime juice for the key lime juice.

Mango-Chili Waffles

Makes 4 (7 in. or 18 cm) round Belgian waffles

MAN, these flavors GO well together. Spiciness and tangy tropical sweetness join forces to create a mouth party. Devour with vanilla dairy-free yogurt or Very Coconutty Syrup (page 130).

> 1 1/2 cups (218 g) all-purpose flour
> 1 cup (140 g) whole wheat flour
> 2 teaspoons baking powder
> 1 teaspoon baking soda
> 1 teaspoon salt
> 2 teaspoons paprika
> 1 teaspoon chili powder
> 1/8 to 1/4 teaspoon ground cayenne (optional)
> 2 cups (475 ml) soy milk or other plant milk
> 1 ripe finely chopped mango (between 3/4 and 1 cup, 170 g, see note)
> 3/4 cup (150 g) sugar
> 1/4 cup plus 2 tablespoons (90 ml) canola or other vegetable oil
> 2 tablespoons lime juice
> 2 teaspoons vanilla extract

Combine the all-purpose flour, whole wheat flour, baking powder, baking soda, salt, paprika, chili powder, and cayenne in a large bowl and stir with a whisk. Thoroughly mix the plant milk, mango, sugar, oil, lime juice, and vanilla extract in a medium bowl. Pour the wet mixture into the flour mixture and stir just until blended.

Preheat the waffle iron according to the manufacturer's directions. Spray both grids generously with oil. Pour or ladle the batter into the center of the iron, covering no more than two-thirds of the iron's surface for the first waffle. Adjust the amount as needed for subsequent waffles. Bake each waffle for 4 to 5 minutes, or until it can be removed easily.

Note: If you don't have a fresh mango, you may substitute 1 cup (170 g) of previously frozen, finely chopped mango.

Orange-Ginger Snap Waffles

Makes 4 (7 in. or 18 cm) round Belgian waffles

These wake up the tongue with a sugary tingle and a refreshing twist of orange. Supplement the mandarin orange bits with vegan whipped topping and candied ginger.

1 cup (189 g) drained mandarin orange slices, finely chopped, divided
1 1/2 cups (218 g) all-purpose flour
1 cup (140 g) whole wheat flour
2 teaspoons baking powder
1 teaspoon baking soda
1 teaspoon salt
1 1/2 teaspoons ground ginger
1 1/4 teaspoons ground cinnamon
1/4 teaspoon ground clove
1 1/4 cups (300 ml) soy milk or other plant milk
3/4 cup (150 g) sugar
1/4 cup plus 2 tablespoons (90 ml) canola or other vegetable oil
1/4 cup (60 ml) molasses
1 teaspoon orange extract
1 teaspoon vanilla extract

Chop the mandarin orange slices and set aside. Combine the all-purpose flour, whole wheat flour, baking powder, baking soda, salt, ginger, cinnamon, and clove in a large bowl and stir with a whisk. Thoroughly mix the plant milk, 1/3 cup (63 g) of the mandarin orange, sugar, oil, molasses, orange extract, and vanilla extract in a medium bowl. Pour the wet mixture into the flour mixture and stir just until blended.

Preheat the waffle iron according to the manufacturer's directions. Spray both grids with oil. Pour or ladle the batter into the center of the iron, covering no more than two-thirds of the iron's surface for the first waffle. Adjust the amount as needed for subsequent waffles. Bake each waffle for 4 to 5 minutes, or until it can be removed easily. Top the waffles with the remaining 2/3 cup (126 g) of mandarin orange.

Anise Biscotti Waffles

Makes 4 (7 in. or 18 cm) round Belgian waffles

Fluffier and more bread-like than the crispy cafe treats, these snacks are delicious dunked in coffee, hot cocoa, tea, or Dark Chocolate Syrup (page 125).

> 1/4 cup (30 g) finely chopped raw almonds
> 1 cup (145 g) all-purpose flour
> 3/4 cup (105 g) whole wheat flour
> 2 teaspoons baking powder
> 1 teaspoon baking soda
> 3/4 teaspoon salt
> 1 tablespoon plus 1 teaspoon non-ground anise seed
> 1 3/4 cups (410 ml) soy milk or other plant milk
> 1 cup (200 g) sugar
> 1/4 cup (60 ml) smooth applesauce
> 1/4 cup (60 ml) canola or other vegetable oil
> 1 1/2 teaspoons anise extract
> 1 teaspoon vanilla extract

Chop the almonds and set aside. Combine the all-purpose flour, whole wheat flour, baking powder, baking soda, salt, and anise seed in a large bowl and stir with a whisk. Thoroughly mix the plant milk, sugar, applesauce, oil, anise extract, and vanilla extract in a medium bowl. Pour the wet mixture into the flour mixture and stir just until blended. Fold in the almonds.

Preheat the waffle iron according to the manufacturer's directions. Spray both grids with oil. Pour or ladle the batter into the center of the iron, covering no more than two-thirds of the iron's surface for the first waffle. Adjust the amount as needed for subsequent waffles. Bake each waffle for 4 to 5 minutes, or until it can be removed easily.

Banana-Blueberry-Teff Waffles (GF)

Makes 4 (7 in. or 18 cm) round Belgian waffles

These deliver whole-grain flavor, slight tartness, and just a little crunch. Liven them up even more with a drizzle of maple syrup, strawberry jam, or Banana-Maple-Nut Syrup (page 126).

> 1 cup (158 g) brown rice flour
> 3/4 cup (105 g) teff flour (different from whole grain teff)
> 2 teaspoons baking powder
> 1 teaspoon baking soda
> 3/4 teaspoon salt
> 1/2 teaspoon xanthan gum powder
> 1 teaspoon ground cinnamon
> 2 ripe medium bananas (2/3 cup, 160 ml, or 180 g peeled and mashed)
> 1 1/2 cups (350 ml) soy milk or other plant milk
> 1/2 cup (120 ml) plain dairy-free yogurt
> 3 tablespoons canola or other vegetable oil
> 2 tablespoons brown sugar
> 1 teaspoon vanilla extract
> 1 cup (148 g) blueberries

Combine the rice flour, teff flour, baking powder, baking soda, salt, xanthan gum powder, and cinnamon in a large bowl and stir with a whisk. Mash the bananas in a medium bowl, and thoroughly mix with the plant milk, dairy-free yogurt, oil, brown sugar, and vanilla extract. Pour the wet mixture into the flour mixture and stir until well blended and any large clumps are gone. Fold in the blueberries. Let stand for 3 to 5 minutes, while preheating the waffle iron according to the manufacturer's directions.

Stir the batter another 5 to 10 strokes, to get rid of any remaining rice flour clumps. Spray both grids of the waffle iron generously with oil. Pour or ladle the batter into the center of the iron, covering no more than two-thirds of the iron's surface for the first waffle. Adjust the amount as needed for subsequent waffles. Bake each waffle for 4 to 5 minutes, or until it can be removed easily.

Crispy Maple-Cashew Waffles (GF)

Makes 4 (7 in. or 18 cm) round Belgian waffles

Relatively basic with just a little flair, these have a high COFI (Crispy Outside and Fluffy Inside) factor. Embellish with additional cashews, Dark Chocolate Syrup (page 125), or Maple Syrup Supreme (page 128).

> 3/4 cup (84 g) raw cashews, finely chopped
> 1 1/4 cups (198 g) brown rice flour
> 1/2 cup (64 g) tapioca flour
> 1/2 cup (70 g) teff flour (different from whole grain teff)
> 2 teaspoons baking powder
> 1 teaspoon baking soda
> 1 1/4 teaspoons salt
> 1 teaspoon xanthan gum powder
> 1/2 teaspoon ground cinnamon (optional)
> 1 3/4 cups (410 ml) soy milk or other plant milk
> 3/4 cup (180 ml) maple syrup
> 1/4 cup plus 2 tablespoons (90 ml) canola or other vegetable oil
> 1 teaspoon lemon juice or cider vinegar
> 1 teaspoon vanilla extract

Chop the cashews and set aside. Combine the rice flour, tapioca flour, teff flour, baking powder, baking soda, salt, xanthan gum powder, and cinnamon in a large bowl and stir with a whisk. Thoroughly mix the plant milk, maple syrup, oil, lemon juice, and vanilla extract in a medium bowl. Pour the wet mixture into the flour mixture and stir until well blended and any large clumps are gone. Fold in the cashews. Let stand for 3 to 5 minutes, while preheating the waffle iron according to the manufacturer's directions.

Stir the batter another 5 to 10 strokes, to get rid of any remaining rice flour clumps. Spray both grids of the waffle iron generously with oil. Pour or ladle the batter into the center of the iron, covering no more than two-thirds of the iron's surface for the first waffle. Adjust the amount as needed for subsequent waffles. Bake each waffle for 3 to 4 minutes, or until it can be removed easily.

Coconut-Date Waffles (GF)

Makes 4 (7 in. or 18 cm) round Belgian waffles

These are chewy and filling, with a slightly macaroonish texture added by the coconut, and the unique sweetness of dates. Enjoy solo, or top with Dark Chocolate Syrup (page 125) or Crazeee Carob Syrup (page 126). Two recipe variations follow.

6 pitted and finely chopped (103 g) Medjool dates
1 1/2 cups (350 ml) full-fat coconut milk
3/4 cup (180 ml) water
1/4 cup (46 g) brown sugar
1/4 cup (22 g) ground flaxseed
1 teaspoon vanilla extract
1 1/2 cups (237 g) brown rice flour
1/2 cup (64 g) tapioca flour
2 teaspoons baking powder
1 teaspoon baking soda
1 teaspoon salt
1 cup (50 g) finely shredded unsweetened coconut (macaroon style)

Chop the dates and set aside. Combine the coconut milk, water, brown sugar, ground flaxseed, and vanilla extract in a medium bowl and whisk until well mixed. Combine the rice flour, tapioca flour, baking powder, baking soda, and salt in a large bowl and stir with a whisk. Pour the wet mixture into the flour mixture and stir until well blended and any large clumps are gone. Fold in the shredded coconut and dates. Let stand for 3 to 5 minutes, while preheating the waffle iron according to the manufacturer's directions.

Stir the batter another 5 to 10 strokes, to get rid of any remaining rice flour clumps. Spray both grids of the waffle iron generously with oil—this is especially important for gluten-free recipes with flaxseed, even if your iron is "non-stick." Pour or ladle the batter into the center of the iron, covering no more than two-thirds of the iron's surface for the first waffle. Adjust the amount as needed for subsequent waffles. Bake each waffle for 4 to 6 minutes, or until it can be removed easily.

Variation #1: Yeasted Coconut Date Waffles (GF)

These have a slightly lighter texture than the original and subtle pleasant overtones added by the fermentation.

Increase water to 1 cup (240 ml) warm water and add 1 1/4 teaspoons active dry yeast.

Dissolve the yeast in the water in a large non-metal bowl. Let stand for 5 minutes. Stir in the rice flour, tapioca flour, and salt until well blended. The mixture will be thick. Cover the bowl and place it in a warm location so the flour mixture can ferment—for at least 3 hours, or 1 1/2 hours if using quick-rise yeast (see "Yeasted Waffle Tips," page 23). Because this is a gluten-free mixture, it may expand only slightly, but the process will add flavor and texture.

Chop the dates and set aside. After the flour mixture has risen, combine the coconut milk, brown sugar, ground flaxseed, vanilla, baking powder, and baking soda in a small bowl. Mix thoroughly, breaking up any clumps. Pour into the fermented flour mixture and stir until well blended. Fold in the dates and shredded coconut. Let stand for 15 minutes, while preheating the waffle iron according to the manufacturer's directions.

Spray both grids of the waffle iron generously with oil—this is especially important for gluten-free recipes with flaxseed, even if your iron is "non-stick." Pour or ladle the batter into the center of the iron, covering no more than two-thirds of the iron's surface for the first waffle. Adjust the amount as needed for subsequent waffles. Bake each waffle for 3 to 5 minutes, or until it can be removed easily.

Variation #2: Xanthan Gum Substitution (GF)

Increase water in original version of Coconut-Date Waffles to 1 1/4 cups (300 ml). Replace flaxseed with 2 teaspoons xanthan gum powder. Follow original directions.

Cider-Banana-Raisin Waffles (GF)

Makes 4 (7 in. or 18 cm) round Belgian waffles

Combining several fruit flavors, these are a bit less sugary than the Cider-Pecan Waffles (page 70) but include the natural sweetness of bananas and raisins. Serve with Banana-Maple-Nut Syrup (page 126) or vanilla dairy-free yogurt.

1 3/4 cups (276 g) brown rice flour
1/2 cup (64 g) tapioca flour
2 teaspoons baking powder
1 teaspoon baking soda
1 teaspoon salt
2 teaspoons xanthan gum powder
1/2 teaspoon ground cinnamon
1 ripe medium banana (1/3 cup, 80 ml, or 90 g peeled and mashed)
1 1/2 cups (350 ml) apple cider
3/4 cup (180 ml) soy milk or other plant milk
1/2 cup (120 ml) canola or other vegetable oil
1/2 cup (100 g) sugar
1 teaspoon vanilla extract
1/3 cup (53 g) raisins

Combine the rice flour, tapioca flour, baking powder, baking soda, salt, xanthan gum powder, and cinnamon in a large bowl and stir with a whisk. Mash the banana in a medium bowl, and thoroughly mix with the apple cider, plant milk, oil, sugar, and vanilla extract. Pour the wet mixture into the flour mixture and stir until well blended and any large clumps are gone. Fold in the raisins. Let stand for 3 to 5 minutes, while preheating the waffle iron according to the manufacturer's directions.

Stir the batter another 5 to 10 strokes, to get rid of any remaining rice flour clumps. Spray both grids generously with oil. Pour or ladle the batter into the center of the iron, covering no more than two-thirds of the iron's surface for the first waffle. Adjust the amount as needed for subsequent waffles. Bake each waffle for 4 to 6 minutes, or until it can be removed easily.

Cashew-Carob-Molasses Waffles (GF)

Makes 4 (7 in. or 18 cm) round Belgian waffles

You just might become possessive after making a batch of these: "I'd better not cashew trying to eat my Cashew-Carob-Molasses Waffles!" They will touch your palate with a moderately sweet, earthy tone. Accompany with Crazeee Carob Syrup (page 126) or Maple Syrup Supreme (page 128).

1/2 cup (56 g) raw cashews, finely chopped
1 1/2 cups (237 g) brown rice flour
1/2 cup (64 g) tapioca flour
1/2 cup (60 g) toasted carob powder
2 teaspoons baking powder
1 teaspoon baking soda
1 1/4 teaspoons salt
1 1/2 teaspoons xanthan gum powder
2 cups (475 ml) soy milk or other plant milk
1/2 cup (100 g) sugar
1/3 cup (80 ml) canola or other vegetable oil
1/4 cup (60 ml) molasses
1 teaspoon vanilla extract

Chop the cashews and set aside. Combine the rice flour, tapioca flour, carob powder, baking powder, baking soda, salt, and xanthan gum powder in a large bowl and stir with a whisk. Thoroughly mix the plant milk, sugar, oil, molasses, and vanilla extract in a medium bowl. Pour the wet mixture into the flour mixture and stir until well blended and any large clumps are gone. Fold in the cashews. Let stand for 3 to 5 minutes, while preheating the waffle iron according to the manufacturer's directions.

Stir the batter another 5 to 10 strokes, to get rid of any remaining rice flour clumps. Spray both grids of the waffle iron generously with oil. Pour or ladle the batter into the center of the iron, covering no more than two-thirds of the iron's surface for the first waffle. Adjust the amount as needed for subsequent waffles. Bake each waffle for 3 to 5 minutes, or until it can be removed easily.

Punkwheat Pumpkin-Buckwheat Waffles (GF)

Makes 5 (7 in. or 18 cm) round Belgian waffles

Punkwheat Waffles are here to rock your kitchen—and your taste buds. They blend sweet, moist wholesomeness with warm spices. While particularly good on a fall or winter day, they are wonderful any time of year. Top with Coconut Whipped Cream (page 148) or, for more spicy warmth, Kicky Waffle Syrup (page 146).

> 2 to 2 1/4 cups (475 to 530 ml) soy milk or other plant milk
>   (see note)
> 1 cup (245 g) canned pureed pumpkin
> 1/4 cup plus 2 tablespoons (69 g) brown sugar
> 1/4 cup (60 ml) canola or other vegetable oil
> 1/4 cup (22 g) ground flaxseed
> 1 tablespoon lemon juice or cider vinegar
> 1 teaspoon vanilla extract
> 1 cup (150 g) buckwheat flour
> 1/2 cup (64 g) tapioca flour
> 1/4 cup (40 g) brown rice flour
> 1 teaspoon baking powder
> 1 teaspoon baking soda
> 1 teaspoon ground cinnamon
> 1 teaspoon salt
> 1/2 teaspoon ground ginger
> 1/8 teaspoon ground nutmeg
> 1/16 to 1/8 teaspoon ground clove (optional)

Combine the plant milk, pumpkin, brown sugar, oil, ground flaxseed, lemon juice, and vanilla extract in a medium bowl and mix thoroughly. Allow to sit for 5 minutes. While the liquid mixture is sitting, combine the buckwheat flour, tapioca flour, rice flour, baking powder, baking soda, cinnamon, salt, ginger, nutmeg, and clove in a large bowl and stir with a whisk.

Pour the liquid mixture into the flour mixture and stir until well blended and any large clumps are gone. Let stand for 3 to 5 minutes, while preheating the waffle maker according to the manufacturer's directions.

Stir the batter another 5 to 10 strokes, to get rid of any remaining flour clumps. Spray both grids of the iron generously with oil—this is especially important for gluten-free recipes with flaxseed, even if your iron is "non-stick." Pour or ladle the batter into the center of the iron, covering no more than two-thirds of the iron's surface for the first waffle. Adjust the amount as needed for subsequent waffles. Bake each waffle for 3 to 5 minutes, or until it can be removed easily.

Notes: Start with 2 cups (475 ml) plant milk. If the first waffle is too dense or not moist enough, add up to 1/4 cup (60 ml) more plant milk to the mix, 1 or 2 tablespoons at a time. Be careful, though, as adding liquid can increase the likelihood of sticking.

Teffinitely Banana-Teff Waffles (GF)

Makes 5 to 6 (7 in. or 18 cm) round Belgian waffles

Between mouthfuls, two non-vegan friends said these were the best waffles they had ever enjoyed. Try a bite of one plain, hot, and fresh; then cover it with chocolate chips, bananas, and maple syrup.

> **1 ripe medium banana (1/3 cup, 80 ml, or 90 g peeled and mashed)**
> **2 cups (475 ml) soy milk or other plant milk**
> **1/4 cup plus 2 tablespoons (69 g) brown sugar**
> **1/4 cup plus 2 tablespoons (90 ml) canola or other vegetable oil**
> **1/4 cup (22 g) ground flaxseed**
> **2 tablespoons molasses**
> **1 1/2 teaspoons vanilla extract**
> **1 1/2 cups (237 g) brown rice flour**
> **1/2 cup (64 g) tapioca flour**
> **1/4 cup (52 g) whole grain teff (different from teff flour)**
> **2 teaspoons baking powder**
> **1 teaspoon baking soda**
> **1 1/4 teaspoons salt**

Mash the banana with a fork or potato masher in a medium bowl. Add the plant milk, brown sugar, oil, ground flaxseed, molasses, and vanilla extract and mix thoroughly. Combine the rice flour, tapioca flour, whole grain teff, baking powder, baking soda, and salt in a large bowl and stir with a whisk. Pour the liquid mixture into the flour mixture and stir until well blended and any large clumps are gone. Let stand for 3 to 5 minutes, while preheating the waffle iron according to the manufacturer's directions.

Stir the batter another 5 to 10 strokes, to get rid of any remaining rice flour clumps. Spray both grids of the iron generously with oil—this is especially important for gluten-free recipes with flaxseed, even if your iron is "non-stick." Pour or ladle the batter into the center of the iron, covering no more than two-thirds of the iron's surface for the first waffle. Adjust the amount as needed for subsequent waffles. Bake each waffle for 3 to 5 minutes, or until it can be removed easily.

Molasses-Tastic Waffles (GF)

Makes 4 (7 in. or 18 cm) round Belgian waffles

These delicious disks were created during a snow and ice storm, when there were few things better to do than bake up hot vegan waffles. They have twice the molasses of the Buckwheat-Molasses Waffles (page 54) and use flaxseed instead of xanthan gum. If you want the toasty, wholesome flavor to shine through, simply top with maple syrup and fruit. To complement the pronounced molasses flavor with something richer, try Dark Chocolate Syrup (page 125) or Crazeee Carob Syrup (page 126).

> 1 1/2 cups (350 ml) soy milk or other plant milk
> 1/4 cup (60 ml) canola or other vegetable oil
> 1/4 cup (22 g) ground flaxseed
> 1/4 cup (60 ml) molasses
> 1 1/4 cups (180 g) buckwheat flour
> 1 cup (128 g) tapioca flour
> 1 1/2 teaspoons baking powder
> 1 teaspoon baking soda
> 1 teaspoon salt

Combine the plant milk, oil, ground flaxseed, and molasses in a medium bowl and whisk until thoroughly mixed. Combine the buckwheat flour, tapioca flour, baking powder, baking soda, and salt in a large bowl and stir or whisk until well blended. Pour the wet ingredients into the dry and stir until well blended and any large clumps are gone. Let stand for 3 to 5 minutes, while preheating the waffle iron according to the manufacturer's directions.

Stir the batter another 5 to 10 strokes, to get rid of any remaining flour clumps. Spray both grids of the iron generously with oil—this is especially important for gluten-free recipes with flaxseed, even if your iron is "non-stick." Pour or ladle the batter into the center of the iron, covering no more than two-thirds of the iron's surface for the first waffle. Adjust the amount as needed for subsequent waffles. Bake each waffle for 3 to 5 minutes, or until it can be removed easily.

Easy Coconut-Almond Waffles (GF)

Makes 3 to 4 (7 in. or 18 cm) round Belgian waffles

Created for those of us who really love almond and coconut, these treats use both coconut sugar and coconut milk. They boast a mild sweetness, crispy outsides, and slightly chewy insides. Top with Coconut Whipped Cream (page 148) and drizzle with maple syrup and chopped almonds.

1 1/2 cups (350 ml) full-fat coconut milk
1/2 cup (120 ml) warm water
1/4 cup (36 g) coconut sugar
1/4 cup (22 g) ground flaxseed
1 1/4 cups (120 g) almond meal
1 cup (158 g) brown rice flour
3/4 cup (128 g) tapioca flour
2 1/4 teaspoons baking powder
1 teaspoon salt

Combine the coconut milk, warm water, coconut sugar, and ground flaxseed in a medium bowl, and whisk until well mixed. Combine the almond meal, rice flour, tapioca flour, baking powder, and salt in a large bowl, and stir or whisk until thoroughly blended. Pour the wet ingredients into the dry and mix until well blended and any large clumps are gone. Allow the batter to stand for 3 to 5 minutes while preheating the waffle iron according to the manufacturer's directions.

Stir the batter another 5 to 10 strokes, breaking up any clumps of flour that haven't absorbed moisture. Spray both grids of the iron generously with oil—this is especially important for gluten-free recipes with flaxseed, even if your iron is "non-stick." Pour or ladle the batter into the center of the iron, covering no more than two-thirds of the iron's surface for the first waffle. Adjust the amount as needed for subsequent waffles. Bake each waffle for 3 to 5 minutes, or until it can be removed easily.

Banana-Almond Delight Waffles (GF)

Makes 4 (7 in. or 18 cm) round Belgian waffles

These culinary concoctions rely upon the oils naturally present in the almonds and coconut, and they utilize the sweetness of brown sugar and banana. Their crispy exteriors accompany moist, banana-laden interiors. Top with sliced bananas and blueberries, or Blueberry Spice Syrup (page 140).

> 1 ripe medium banana (1/3 cup, 80 ml, or 90 g peeled and mashed)
> 1 cup (240 ml) warm water
> 1 1/2 cups (350 ml) full-fat coconut milk
> 1/4 cup (22 g) ground flaxseed
> 2 tablespoons brown sugar
> 1 cup (100 g) almond meal
> 1 cup (158 g) brown rice flour
> 1/2 cup (64 g) tapioca flour
> 2 1/4 teaspoons baking powder
> 1 teaspoon salt

Mash the banana in a medium bowl. Add the warm water, coconut milk, ground flaxseed, and brown sugar and whisk until well mixed. Combine the almond meal, rice flour, tapioca flour, baking powder, and salt in a large bowl and stir or whisk until thoroughly blended.

Pour the wet ingredients into the dry and mix until blended. The batter should be only slightly lumpy, with lumps smaller than peas. Allow the batter to stand for 3 to 5 minutes while preheating the waffle iron according to the manufacturer's directions.

Stir the batter another 5 to 10 strokes, breaking up any clumps of rice flour that haven't absorbed moisture. Spray both grids of the iron generously with oil—this is especially important for gluten-free recipes with flaxseed, even if your iron is "non-stick." Pour or ladle the batter into the center of the iron, covering no more than two-thirds of the iron's surface for the first waffle. Adjust the amount as needed for subsequent waffles. Bake each waffle for 3 to 5 minutes, or until it can be removed easily.

Gluten-Free Dark Chocolate Cake Waffles (GF)

Makes 4 (7 in. or 18 cm) round Belgian waffles

These are a fun, rich, and equally delicious alternative to the original wheat flour version (page 67). Enjoy with Cocoa or Carob Agave Nectar (page 127), Coco Kah-banana Syrup (page 129), or Creamy Maple-Chai Dream Sauce (page 133). Or, top with fresh strawberries, raspberries, or your favorite fruit preserves.

> 2 cups (475 ml) soy milk or other plant milk
> 3/4 cup (180 ml) canola or other vegetable oil
> 1/2 cup plus 2 tablespoons (115 g) brown sugar
> 1/4 cup (22 g) ground flaxseed
> 1 1/2 teaspoons vanilla extract
> 1 1/2 cups (237 g) brown rice flour
> 1/2 cup (64 g) tapioca flour
> 1/2 cup (44 g) cocoa powder
> 1 1/2 teaspoons baking powder
> 1 teaspoon baking soda
> 1 teaspoon salt

Combine the plant milk, oil, brown sugar, ground flaxseed, and vanilla in a medium bowl, and whisk until well mixed. Combine the rice flour, tapioca flour, cocoa powder, baking powder, baking soda, and salt in a large bowl, and stir or whisk until thoroughly blended. Pour the wet ingredients into the dry and mix until well blended and any large clumps are gone. If necessary, use a spoon or spatula to break up any cocoa clumps and push the cocoa down into the batter. Allow the batter to stand for 3 to 5 minutes while preheating the waffle iron according to the manufacturer's directions.

Stir the batter another 5 to 10 strokes, breaking up any clumps of flour that haven't absorbed moisture. Spray both grids of the iron generously with oil—this is especially important for gluten-free recipes with flaxseed, even if your iron is "non-stick." Pour or ladle the batter into the center of the iron, covering no more than two-thirds of the iron's surface for the first waffle. Adjust the amount as needed for subsequent waffles. Bake each waffle for 3 to 5 minutes, or until it can be removed easily.

Flavory-Savory Waffles

These waffles make heavy use of herbs, spices, and various fillings or mix-ins, alongside minimal to moderate levels of sweetness. You can enjoy them just as they are, with a very simple topping such as vegan butter, or with the suggested toppings that complement their flavors. For example, the Refried Bean, Rice, and Cornmeal Waffles (page 117) can serve as a snack of their own, but also call out for salsa, cheese-like sauces, and vegan sour cream. The Carrot-Ginger-Sage Waffles (page 94) welcome a bit of sweetness to join the warmth and savoriness.

Spicy Blue Tortilla Chip Waffles

Makes 4 (7 in. or 18 cm) round Belgian waffles

Torti-yeeeah, I like these! Their taste resembles that of a spicy cheesy tortilla chip, free of the milk-based additives. Of course, they're also much fluffier and less crunchy. Eat solo or top with salsa, vegan sour cream, or black beans.

> 1 cup (68 g) crumbled blue or other color tortilla chips, broken into
>   pieces smaller than a thumbnail
> 1 cup (145 g) all-purpose flour
> 1/2 cup (70 g) whole wheat flour
> 1/2 cup (85 g) cornmeal
> 2 teaspoons baking powder
> 1 teaspoon baking soda
> 1 1/2 teaspoons salt
> 1/2 cup (30 g) nutritional yeast flakes
> 1 1/2 teaspoons onion powder
> 1 1/4 teaspoons garlic powder
> 1/8 teaspoon ground cayenne
> 2 cups plus 1 tablespoon (490 ml) soy milk or other plant milk
> 1/2 cup plus 2 tablespoons (150 ml) canola or other vegetable oil
> 3 tablespoons sugar
> 2 tablespoons lime juice

Crumble the tortilla chips and set aside. Combine the all-purpose flour, whole wheat flour, cornmeal, baking powder, baking soda, salt, nutritional yeast, onion powder, garlic powder, and cayenne in a large bowl and stir with a whisk. Thoroughly mix the plant milk, oil, sugar, and lime juice in a medium bowl. Pour the wet mixture into the flour mixture and stir just until blended. Fold in the crumbled corn chips.

Preheat the waffle iron according to the manufacturer's directions. Spray both grids with oil. Pour or ladle the batter into the center of the iron, covering no more than two-thirds of the iron's surface for the first waffle. Adjust the amount as needed for subsequent waffles. Bake each waffle for 4 to 5 minutes, or until it can be removed easily.

Carrot-Ginger-Sage Waffles

Makes 4 (7 in. or 18 cm) round Belgian waffles

Overtones of sage blend with just enough gingery snap to warm the palate, while carrots add another level of texture. Top with warm spoonfuls of Lemon-Ginger Drizzle (page 130) and bits of candied ginger.

    1 1/4 cups (130 g) grated carrots
    3/4 cup (109 g) all-purpose flour
    3/4 cup (105 g) whole wheat flour
    1 1/2 teaspoons baking powder
    1 teaspoon baking soda
    1 teaspoon salt
    1 tablespoon plus 1 teaspoon rubbed sage
    1 1/2 teaspoons ground ginger
    1 1/2 cups (350 ml) soy milk or other plant milk
    1/4 cup plus 2 tablespoons (69 g) brown sugar
    1/4 cup (60 ml) canola or other vegetable oil
    3 tablespoons lemon juice

Grate the carrots and set aside. Combine the all-purpose flour, whole wheat flour, baking powder, baking soda, salt, sage, and ginger in a large bowl and stir with a whisk. Thoroughly mix the carrots, plant milk, brown sugar, oil, and lemon juice in a medium bowl. Pour the wet mixture into the flour mixture and stir just until blended.

Preheat the waffle iron according to the manufacturer's directions. Spray both grids with oil. Pour or ladle the batter into the center of the iron, covering no more than two-thirds of the iron's surface for the first waffle. Adjust the amount as needed for subsequent waffles. Bake each waffle for 3 to 5 minutes, or until it can be removed easily.

Spicy Carrot-Raisin Waffles

Makes 3 to 4 (7 in. or 18 cm) round Belgian waffles

Inspired by the carrot salads sometimes offered in Indian restaurants, these make for a slightly spicy-sweet treat. Garnish with spoonfuls of Mint Raita (page 154).

1 1/4 cups (130 g) grated carrots
3/4 cup (109 g) all-purpose flour
3/4 cup (105 g) whole wheat flour
1 1/2 teaspoons baking powder
1 teaspoon baking soda
1 1/4 teaspoons salt
1/8 teaspoon freshly ground black pepper
1/8 teaspoon ground cayenne
1 1/4 cups plus 2 tablespoons (330 ml) soy milk or other plant milk
1/4 cup plus 2 tablespoons (90 ml) olive or other vegetable oil
1/4 cup (12 g) finely chopped fresh chives
2 tablespoons lemon juice
2 tablespoons sugar
1/2 cup (80 g) raisins

Grate the carrots and set aside. Combine the all-purpose flour, whole wheat flour, baking powder, baking soda, salt, black pepper, and cayenne in a large bowl and stir with a whisk. Thoroughly mix the carrots, plant milk, oil, chives, lemon juice, and sugar in a medium bowl. Pour the wet mixture into the flour mixture and stir just until blended. Fold in the raisins.

Preheat the waffle iron according to the manufacturer's directions. Spray both grids with oil. Pour or ladle the batter into the center of the iron, covering no more than two-thirds of the iron's surface for the first waffle. Adjust the amount as needed for subsequent waffles. Bake each waffle for 4 to 5 minutes, or until it can be removed easily.

Orange-Basil-Cornmeal Waffles

Makes 3 to 4 (7 in. or 18 cm) round Belgian waffles

These sophisticated waffles blend subtle sweetness with overtones of toastedness. Top with Coconut-Cashew-Basil Sauce (page 152) or Basil-Orange Vegan Ice Cream (page 138). Because the batter needs time to rise, begin at least 3 hours in advance of baking or 1 1/2 hours in advance if you are using quick-rise yeast.

> 1 1/4 teaspoons active dry yeast
> 1 1/2 cups (350 ml) warm orange juice (see "Yeasted Waffle Tips,"
>   page 23)
> 1 1/2 cups (218 g) all-purpose flour
> 3/4 cup (128 g) cornmeal
> 1 teaspoon salt
> 1/3 cup (9 g) packed fresh basil, finely chopped
> 1/4 cup plus 2 tablespoons (90 ml) soy milk or other plant milk
> 1/4 cup (60 ml) canola or other vegetable oil
> 1/4 cup (50 g) sugar
> 1 1/2 teaspoons baking powder
> 1 teaspoon vanilla extract

Dissolve the yeast in the warm orange juice in a large non-metal bowl. Let stand for 5 minutes. Stir in the all-purpose flour, cornmeal, and salt until well blended. Cover the bowl and place it in a warm location until the flour mixture has almost doubled (see "Yeasted Waffle Tips," page 23).

After the flour mixture has risen, combine the basil, plant milk, oil, sugar, baking powder, and vanilla extract in a medium bowl. Thoroughly mix, breaking up any clumps of baking powder. Pour into the raised flour mixture and stir until well blended. Let stand for 15 minutes, while preheating the waffle iron according to the manufacturer's directions.

Spray both grids of the waffle iron with oil. Pour or ladle the batter into the center of the iron, covering no more than two-thirds of the iron's surface for the first waffle. Adjust the amount as needed for subsequent waffles. Bake each waffle for 4 to 6 minutes, or until it can be removed easily.

Cheddar Cheesy Waffles

Makes 4 (7 in. or 18 cm) round Belgian waffles

Suited for a snack or a meal, these are reminiscent of savory and salty cheese-flavored crackers—except they're vegan and 100 times as large. Serve solo, with Southwestern Beans and Greens (page 156), or with applesauce.

> 1 cup (145 g) all-purpose flour
> 1/2 cup (70 g) whole wheat flour
> 1/2 cup (56 g) rolled oats
> 2 teaspoons baking powder
> 1 teaspoon baking soda
> 3/4 teaspoon salt
> 3 tablespoons nutritional yeast flakes
> 1 teaspoon onion powder
> 1/2 teaspoon paprika
> 1/4 teaspoon garlic powder
> 1/4 teaspoon dry mustard powder
> 2 cups (475 ml) soy milk or other plant milk
> 1/4 cup (60 ml) canola or other vegetable oil
> 2 tablespoons sugar
> 2 tablespoons lemon juice
> 1 tablespoon plus 2 teaspoons light or chickpea miso
> 1 tablespoon prepared horseradish (optional)

Combine the all-purpose flour, whole wheat flour, oats, baking powder, baking soda, salt, nutritional yeast, onion powder, paprika, garlic powder, and mustard powder in a large bowl and stir with a whisk. Thoroughly mix the plant milk, oil, sugar, lemon juice, miso, and horseradish in a medium bowl. Break up any clumps of miso. Pour the wet mixture into the flour mixture and stir just until blended. Let stand for 4 to 5 minutes, while preheating the waffle iron according to the manufacturer's directions.

Spray both grids of the waffle iron with oil. Pour or ladle the batter into the center of the iron, covering no more than two-thirds of the iron's surface for the first waffle. Adjust the amount as needed for subsequent waffles. Bake each waffle for 4 to 5 minutes, or until it can be removed easily.

Refried Bean & Cornmeal Waffles

Makes 5 (7 in. or 18 cm) round Belgian waffles

Have you ever wondered what might happen if you tried to combine a whole Mexican meal in a waffle iron? Lime, cumin, and cayenne lend a south of the border style. Top with salsa, guacamole, vegan sour cream, and vegan cheese.

> 3/4 cup (109 g) all-purpose flour
> 3/4 cup (105 g) whole wheat flour
> 3/4 cup (128 g) cornmeal
> 2 teaspoons baking powder
> 1 teaspoon baking soda
> 1 teaspoon salt (see note)
> 1 3/4 teaspoons ground cumin
> 1 teaspoon onion powder
> 1/8 teaspoon ground cayenne
> 1 1/2 cups (350 ml) soy milk or other plant milk
> 1 can (15 oz./425 g) refried black beans, drained and rinsed
> 1/4 cup plus 2 tablespoons (90 ml) canola or other vegetable oil
> 3 tablespoons lime juice
> 3 tablespoons sugar

Combine the all-purpose flour, whole wheat flour, cornmeal, baking powder, baking soda, salt, cumin, onion powder, and cayenne in a large bowl and stir with a whisk. Thoroughly mix the plant milk, beans, oil, lime juice, and sugar in a medium bowl. Pour the wet mixture into the flour mixture and stir just until blended.

Preheat the waffle iron according to the manufacturer's directions. Spray both grids with oil. Pour or ladle the batter into the center of the iron, covering no more than two-thirds of the iron's surface for the first waffle. Adjust the amount as needed for subsequent waffles. Bake each waffle for 4 to 6 minutes, or until it can be removed easily.

Note: Reduce the salt to 3/4 teaspoon or less if beans are heavily salted.

Banana-Fofana-Walnut Waffles

Makes 4 (7 in. or 18 cm) round Belgian waffles

The airy texture of spelt is married to gentle spice and sweetness. I sometimes dream about these waffles and wake up gnawing on the corner of my pillow. They make great partners for Banana-Maple-Nut Syrup (page 126) or just warm maple syrup.

1/3 cup (40 g) finely chopped raw walnuts
1 3/4 cups (271 g) spelt flour
1/2 cup (56 g) rolled oats
2 teaspoons baking powder
3/4 teaspoon salt
1 1/2 teaspoons ground cinnamon
3/4 teaspoon ground or grated nutmeg
1/2 teaspoon ground ginger
1 ripe medium banana (1/3 cup, 80 ml, or 90 g peeled and mashed)
2 1/4 cups (530 ml) soy milk or other plant milk
3 tablespoons canola or other vegetable oil
2 tablespoons ground flaxseed
1 teaspoon vanilla extract

Chop the walnuts and set aside. Combine the flour, oats, baking powder, salt, cinnamon, nutmeg, and ginger in a large bowl and stir with a whisk. Mash the banana in a medium bowl, and thoroughly mix with the plant milk, oil, flaxseed, and vanilla extract. Pour the wet mixture into the flour mixture and stir just until blended. Fold in the walnuts. Let stand for 6 to 7 minutes, while preheating the waffle iron according to the manufacturer's directions.

Spray both grids of the waffle iron generously with oil. Pour or ladle the batter into the center of the iron, covering no more than two-thirds of the iron's surface for the first waffle. Adjust the amount as needed for subsequent waffles. Bake each waffle for 4 to 5 minutes, or until it can be removed easily.

Umami Mama Waffles: The Mother of Savory

Makes 4 (7 in. or 18 cm) round Belgian waffles

This isn't the name of an Abba musical, but these pizza-like waffles should make your taste buds sing. Savor them as they are, or create perfect harmony with the Savory Cashew-Mushroom Sauce (page 151). Because the batter needs time to rise, begin at least 3 hours in advance of baking or 1 1/2 hours in advance if you are using quick-rise yeast.

> 1 1/4 teaspoons active dry yeast
> 1 1/2 cups (350 ml) warm water (see "Yeasted Waffle Tips," page 23)
> 1 cup (145 g) all-purpose flour
> 1 cup (140 g) whole wheat flour
> 3/4 teaspoon salt
> 1/3 cup (56 g) pitted and finely chopped Kalamata olives
> 1/3 cup (71 g) finely chopped sun-dried tomatoes, preserved in olive
>   oil or rehydrated
> 1 cup (240 ml) soy milk or other plant milk
> 1/4 cup (60 ml) olive or other vegetable oil
> 3 tablespoons nutritional yeast flakes
> 1 tablespoon plus 1 teaspoon light or chickpea miso
> 1 tablespoon ground flaxseed
> 1 tablespoon sugar
> 2 medium cloves garlic, crushed
> 1 teaspoon baking powder
> 1 teaspoon dried basil
> 1 teaspoon onion powder
> 1 teaspoon dried oregano
> 1/8 teaspoon ground cayenne (optional)

Dissolve the yeast in the water in a large non-metal bowl. Let stand for 5 minutes. Stir in the all-purpose flour, whole wheat flour, and salt until well blended. Cover the bowl and place it in a warm location until the flour mixture has almost doubled (see "Yeasted Waffle Tips," page 23).

After the flour mixture has risen, chop the olives and sun-dried tomatoes, and set aside. Combine the plant milk, oil, nutritional yeast, miso, flaxseed, sugar, garlic, baking powder, basil, onion powder, oregano, and cayenne in a medium bowl. Mix thoroughly, breaking up any clumps of miso. Pour into the raised flour mixture and stir until well blended. Fold in the olives and sun-dried tomatoes.

Let stand for 15 minutes, while preheating the waffle iron according to the manufacturer's directions.

Spray both grids of the waffle iron generously with oil. Pour or ladle the batter into the center of the iron, covering no more than two-thirds of the iron's surface for the first waffle. Adjust the amount as needed for subsequent waffles. Bake each waffle for 4 to 6 minutes, or until it can be removed easily.

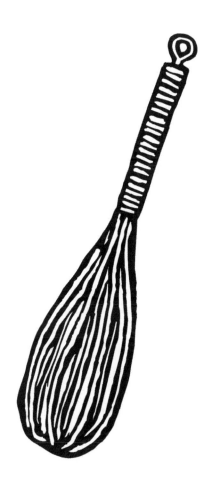

Caramelized Onion & Garlic Waffles

Makes 3 to 4 (7 in. or 18 cm) round Belgian waffles

This is a classic flavor combination, adapted to the exciting world of vegan waffles. Top with You Make Miso Tangy Dipping Sauce (page 153), pizza sauce, or melted vegan cheese. Because the batter needs time to rise, begin at least 3 hours in advance of baking or 1 1/2 hours in advance if you are using quick-rise yeast.

> 1 1/4 teaspoons active dry yeast
> 1 1/2 cups (350 ml) warm water (see "Yeasted Waffle Tips," page 23)
> 1 cup (145 g) all-purpose flour
> 1 cup (140 g) whole wheat flour
> 1 1/2 teaspoons salt
> 1 cup (118 g) finely chopped onion
> 3 medium cloves garlic, crushed
> 1/4 cup plus 2 tablespoons (90 ml) olive or other vegetable oil, divided
> 1/4 cup plus 2 tablespoons (90 ml) soy milk or other plant milk
> 2 tablespoons plain dairy-free yogurt
> 2 tablespoons sugar
> 1/2 teaspoon baking powder
> 1/2 teaspoon baking soda
> 1/4 teaspoon freshly ground black pepper
> 1/8 teaspoon ground cayenne (optional)

Dissolve the yeast in the water in a large non-metal bowl. Let stand for 5 minutes. Stir in the all-purpose flour, whole wheat flour, and salt until well blended. Cover the bowl and place it in a warm location until the flour mixture has almost doubled (see "Yeasted Waffle Tips," page 23).

After the flour mixture has risen, chop the onion. Combine it with the garlic and 2 tablespoons of the oil in a medium frying pan. Sauté over medium heat for about 5 minutes, or just until the onions have softened and the garlic has started to brown. Remove from heat and set aside.

Combine the remaining 1/4 cup (60 ml) of oil, plant milk, dairy-free yogurt, sugar, baking powder, baking soda, black pepper, and cayenne in a medium bowl. Mix thoroughly, breaking up any clumps of baking powder or baking soda. Pour into the raised flour mixture and stir until well blended. Fold in the onions and garlic.

Let stand for 15 minutes, while preheating the waffle iron according to the manufacturer's directions.

Spray both grids of the waffle iron with oil. Pour or ladle the batter into the center of the iron, covering no more than two-thirds of the iron's surface for the first waffle. Adjust the amount as needed for subsequent waffles. Bake each waffle for 4 to 6 minutes, or until it can be removed easily.

Chili-Lime Felafel Waffles

Makes 3 (7 in. or 18 cm) dense round Belgian waffles

Like traditional felafel, these are dense and filling with a bit of a kick; but they incorporate a slight twist in spices. Top with tomatoes, cucumbers, and Cilantro-Lime Tahini Sauce (page 152), and serve on a bed of leafy greens.

> 2 cans (15 oz./425 g each) chickpeas, drained and rinsed
>   (about 3 cups/700 ml)
> 1/2 cup (140 g) whole wheat or (145 g) all-purpose flour
> 1/4 cup plus 2 tablespoons (90 ml) lime juice
> 1/4 cup plus 2 tablespoons (90 ml) olive or other vegetable oil
> 1/4 cup (60 ml) water
> 4 medium cloves garlic
> 2 tablespoons sugar
> 1 tablespoon chili powder
> 2 teaspoons ground cumin
> 1 teaspoon ground coriander
> 1 teaspoon onion powder
> 1 teaspoon salt
> 1 teaspoon xanthan gum powder
> 1/8 to 1/4 teaspoon ground cayenne
> 1 1/2 teaspoons baking powder
> 1 teaspoon baking soda

Place all the ingredients into a food processor or powerful blender, adding the baking powder and baking soda last. Process until smooth or until few small clumps remain (see note).

Preheat the waffle iron according to the manufacturer's directions. Spray both grids with oil. Pour or ladle the batter into the center of the iron, covering no more than two-thirds of the iron's surface for the first waffle. Adjust the amount as needed for subsequent waffles. Bake each waffle for 4 to 6 minutes, or until it can be removed easily.

Note: You may need to process the batter in 2 or 3 smaller portions and then stir them together by hand, especially if using a blender.

Spanakowafflita

Makes 4 (7 in. or 18 cm) round Belgian waffles

Spanako-what? Don't worry about the name because it's not good to talk with a full mouth anyway. These are reminiscent of the spanakopita or spinach pies often served at Greek food festivals, minus the dairy. They can be eaten as a main course for lunch or dinner, and they blend well with the Savory Cashew-Mushroom Sauce (page 151).

> 2 1/2 cups (90 g) packed fresh spinach, finely chopped (see note)
> 1/2 cup (18 g) packed fresh parsley, finely chopped (see note)
> 3 green onions, finely chopped
> 1 1/2 cups (210 g) whole wheat flour
> 1/2 cup (73 g) all-purpose flour
> 2 teaspoons baking powder
> 1 teaspoon baking soda
> 3/4 teaspoon salt
> 1 teaspoon onion powder
> 1/8 teaspoon ground cayenne
> 2 cups (475 ml) soy milk or other plant milk
> 1/4 cup (60 ml) olive or other vegetable oil
> 2 tablespoons light or chickpea miso
> 1 tablespoon ground flaxseed
> 1 tablespoon sugar
> 1 tablespoon white or red wine vinegar, lemon juice, or cider vinegar
> 2 medium cloves garlic, crushed

Chop the spinach, parsley, and onions, and set aside. Combine the whole wheat flour, all-purpose flour, baking powder, baking soda, salt, onion powder, and cayenne in a large bowl and stir with a whisk. Thoroughly mix the plant milk, oil, miso, flaxseed, sugar, vinegar, and garlic in a medium bowl. Break up any clumps of miso. Pour the wet mixture into the flour mixture and stir just until blended. Fold in the chopped spinach, parsley, and onions.

Preheat the waffle iron according to the manufacturer's directions. Spray both grids with oil. Pour or ladle the batter into the center of the iron, covering no more than two-thirds of the iron's surface for the first waffle. Adjust the amount as needed for subsequent waffles. Bake each waffle for 5 to 6 minutes, or until it can be removed easily.

Note: The spinach and parsley should be chopped into pieces no larger than a thumbnail. If they are not chopped finely enough, the waffles will be more likely to separate in the middle upon opening the iron. As an emergency measure, you can add 1/4 to 1/2 teaspoon xanthan gum powder.

Kale-idoscopic Waffles

Makes 4 (7 in. or 18 cm) round Belgian waffles

Staring at a round waffle is somewhat like looking into a kaleidoscope, because the 4 quadrants are nearly mirror images of one another. Don't spend too much time gazing at one of these, though, because it is tastiest while it's hot. A peanutty-spicy blend accents bits of nutritious green kale. Top with Simple Piña Colada-ish Topping (page 134), bits of juicy pineapple, or slices of sautéed onion.

> 3 cups (94 g) packed fresh kale, leaf stems removed before measuring,
>   finely chopped (any variety, see note)
> 1 1/2 cups (210 g) whole wheat flour
> 1/2 cup (73 g) all-purpose flour
> 2 teaspoons baking powder
> 1/2 teaspoon baking soda
> 1 1/2 teaspoons onion powder
> 1/8 teaspoon ground cayenne (optional)
> 2 1/4 cups (530 ml) soy milk or other plant milk
> 1/2 cup (128 g) smooth peanut butter (see note)
> 3 tablespoons soy sauce
> 3 tablespoons sugar
> 2 tablespoons ground flaxseed
> 1 tablespoon cider vinegar
> 2 medium cloves garlic, crushed

Chop the kale and set aside. Combine the whole wheat flour, all-purpose flour, baking powder, baking soda, onion powder, and cayenne in a large bowl and stir with a whisk. Thoroughly mix the plant milk, peanut butter, soy sauce, sugar, ground flaxseed, vinegar, and garlic in a medium bowl. Break up any clumps of peanut butter. Pour the wet mixture into the flour mixture and stir just until blended. Fold in the kale.

Let stand for 3 to 4 minutes, while preheating the waffle iron according to the manufacturer's directions.

Spray both grids of the waffle iron with oil. Pour or ladle the batter into the center of the iron, covering no more than two-thirds of the iron's surface for the first waffle. Adjust the amount as needed for subsequent waffles. Before closing the iron, manually spread the batter out slightly with the ladle or a spatula if needed so the kale doesn't all get stuck near the center. Bake each waffle for 4 to 5 minutes, or until it can be removed easily.

Notes: The kale should be chopped into pieces no larger than your thumbnail. If it is not chopped finely enough, the waffles will be more likely to separate in the middle upon opening the iron.

If you're using peanut butter that has been refrigerated, warming it in the microwave may make it easier to mix into the batter.

Avocado-Pecan Waffles for Two

Makes 2 (7 in. or 18 cm) round Belgian waffles

The subtle but delicious flavors in these waffles go best with plain or vanilla dairy-free yogurt, applesauce, or Raspberry-Avocado Cream (page 126). Enjoy with a friend, or eat both if you're extra hungry.

1/4 cup (30 g) finely chopped raw pecans
3/4 cup (109 g) all-purpose flour
1/4 cup (35 g) whole wheat flour
1 1/4 teaspoon baking powder
1/2 teaspoon baking soda
1/2 teaspoon salt
1/4 teaspoon ground or grated nutmeg
1 ripe medium avocado, mashed until smooth (2/3 to 3/4 cup, 175 ml, or 163 g without peel or pit)
1/2 cup (120 ml) soy milk or other plant milk
1/4 cup plus 1 tablespoon (63 g) sugar
1/4 cup (60 ml) water
2 tablespoons canola or other vegetable oil
2 tablespoons lime juice

Chop the pecans and set aside. Combine the all-purpose flour, whole wheat flour, baking powder, baking soda, salt, and nutmeg in a large bowl and stir with a whisk. Mash the avocado in a medium bowl, and thoroughly mix with the plant milk, sugar, water, oil, and lime juice. Pour the wet mixture into the flour mixture and stir just until blended. Fold in the pecans.

Preheat the waffle iron according to the manufacturer's directions. Spray both grids with oil. Pour or ladle the batter into the center of the iron, covering no more than two-thirds of the iron's surface for the first waffle. Adjust the amount as needed for subsequent waffles. Bake each waffle for 4 to 5 minutes, or until it can be removed easily.

Yeast-Raised Cornmeal Chili-Dippin' Waffles

Makes 4 (7 in. or 18 cm) round Belgian waffles.

These crispy waffles have a subtler sweetness than the average cornbread, with the uncommon addition of sourdough-like overtones. Because the batter needs time to rise, begin at least 3 hours in advance of baking or 1 1/2 hours in advance if you are using quick-rise yeast. Along with chili, these blend well with the Spicy Sloppy Tofu and Portabella (page 158) or the Southwestern Beans and Greens (page 156).

> 1 1/4 teaspoons active dry yeast
> 1 1/2 cups (350 ml) warm water (see "Yeasted Waffle Tips," page 23)
> 3/4 cup (109 g) all-purpose flour
> 1/2 cup (70 g) whole wheat flour
> 3/4 cup (128 g) cornmeal
> 1 1/2 teaspoons salt
> 1/2 cup (120 ml) soy milk or other plant milk
> 1/4 cup plus 2 tablespoons (90 ml) canola or other vegetable oil
> 1/4 cup (46 g) brown sugar
> 2 tablespooons molasses
> 1/2 teaspoon baking powder
> 1/2 teaspoon baking soda

Dissolve the yeast in the water in a large non-metal bowl. Let stand for 5 minutes. Stir in the all-purpose flour, whole wheat flour, cornmeal, and salt until well blended. Cover the bowl and place it in a warm location until the flour mixture has almost doubled (see "Yeasted Waffle Tips," page 23).

After the flour mixture has risen, combine the plant milk, oil, brown sugar, molasses, baking powder, and baking soda in a small bowl. Mix thoroughly, breaking up any clumps of baking powder or baking soda. Pour into the raised flour mixture and stir until well blended. Let stand for 15 minutes, while preheating the waffle iron according to the manufacturer's directions.

Spray both grids of the waffle iron with oil. Pour or ladle the batter into the center of the iron, covering no more than two-thirds of the iron's surface for the first waffle. Adjust the amount as needed for subsequent waffles. Bake each waffle for 3 to 5 minutes, or until it can be removed easily.

Quinoa-Full Keen Waffles

Makes 4 (7 in. or 18 cm) round Belgian waffles

This waffle sports 2 different textures of an ancient super seed, with the chewiness and occasional crunch of whole quinoa adding texture and contrast. Drizzle with warm almond butter or maple syrup.

1/4 cup plus 2 tablespoons (71 g) quinoa seed (also called quinoa grain; see note)
1/4 cup plus 3 tablespoons (105 ml) water
1/2 cup plus 1 teaspoon (125 ml) canola or other vegetable oil, divided
1 1/2 cups (168 g) quinoa flour
1/2 cup (64 g) tapioca flour
2 teaspoons baking powder
1 teaspoon baking soda
1 teaspoon salt
3/4 teaspoon xanthan gum powder
1/2 teaspoon ground cinnamon
1/2 teaspoon ground or grated nutmeg
2 cups (475 ml) soy milk or other plant milk
1/4 cup plus 2 tablespoons (90 ml) maple syrup
1 teaspoon lemon juice or cider vinegar
1/4 cup (40 g) raisins

Place the quinoa seed in a small saucepan with the water and 1 teaspoon of the oil. Cover and heat just until boiling. Then stir, reduce heat, and simmer covered for another 10 minutes. Turn off heat and let stand covered for 5 minutes.

While the quinoa seed is simmering or standing, combine the quinoa flour, tapioca flour, baking powder, baking soda, salt, xanthan gum powder, cinnamon, and nutmeg in a large bowl and stir with a whisk. Thoroughly mix the remaining 1/2 cup (120 ml) of oil, plant milk, maple syrup, and lemon juice in a medium bowl. Pour the wet mixture into the flour mixture and stir just until blended. Fold in the cooked quinoa seed and the raisins.

Preheat the waffle iron according to the manufacturer's directions. Spray both grids with oil. Pour or ladle the batter into the center of the iron, covering no more than two-thirds of the iron's surface for the first waffle. Adjust the amount as needed for subsequent waffles. Bake each waffle for 4 to 5 minutes, or until it can be removed easily.

Note: Prior to cooking, place a few pieces of the whole quinoa seed on your tongue. If you detect a strong bitterness, follow the suggestions under "Quinoa Seed and Flour" (page 26).

Keen Zucchini-Dill Waffles

Makes 4 (7 in. or 18 cm) round Belgian waffles

When midsummer brings an abundance of fresh zucchini, just make waffles out of them. The dill adds to the refreshing zucchini flavor, and the cashews provide richness. Top with plain or vanilla dairy-free yogurt and a twist of lemon juice.

1 1/2 cups (200 g) grated zucchini
1/2 cup (56 g) raw cashews, finely chopped
1/4 cup plus 1 tablespoon (10 g) finely chopped fresh dill
1 cup (145 g) all-purpose flour
1 cup (140 g) whole wheat flour
2 teaspoons baking powder
1 teaspoon baking soda
1 1/2 teaspoons salt
2 tablespoons nutritional yeast flakes
1/2 teaspoon freshly ground black pepper
1 3/4 cups (410 ml) soy milk or other plant milk
1/4 cup plus 2 tablespoons (90 ml) canola or other vegetable oil
1/4 cup plus 2 tablespoons (75 g) sugar
2 tablespoons lemon juice

Grate the zucchini, chop the cashews, chop the dill, and set them aside. Combine the all-purpose flour, whole wheat flour, baking powder, baking soda, salt, nutritional yeast, and pepper in a large bowl and stir with a whisk. Thoroughly mix the zucchini, dill, plant milk, oil, sugar, and lemon juice in a medium bowl. Pour the wet mixture into the flour mixture and stir just until blended. Fold in the cashews.

Preheat the waffle iron according to the manufacturer's directions. Spray both grids with oil. Pour or ladle the batter into the center of the iron, covering no more than two-thirds of the iron's surface for the first waffle. Adjust the amount as needed for subsequent waffles. Bake each waffle for 4 to 6 minutes, or until it can be removed easily.

Some Awesome Samosa Waffles

Makes 4 (7 in. or 18 cm) round Belgian waffles

These are a tribute to the flavorfully stuffed pastry pockets served at Indian restaurants. Raisins add modest sweetness to a tongue-tingling combination of spices. Enjoy with a few spoonfuls of Mint Raita (page 154).

1 cup (194 g) peeled, cooked, drained, and thoroughly mashed
    potatoes, nothing added (roughly 2 medium potatoes)
1/2 cup (80 g) green peas (may be canned or thawed from frozen)
2 tablespoons finely chopped raw cashews
1 cup (140 g) whole wheat flour
1/2 cup (73 g) all-purpose flour
2 teaspoons baking powder
1 teaspoon baking soda
1 1/4 teaspoons salt
2 teaspoons ground coriander
1 1/2 teaspoons garam masala powder
1 teaspoon ground ginger
1 teaspoon onion powder
2 cups (475 ml) soy milk or other plant milk
1/4 cup (60 ml) canola or other vegetable oil
3 tablespoons sugar
2 tablespoons lemon juice
1 medium clove garlic, crushed
2 tablespoons raisins

Place the potatoes in a pot of boiling water or in the microwave, cooking them until they're soft enough to mash easily. While the potatoes are cooking, chop the cashews and set aside. Combine the whole wheat flour, all-purpose flour, baking powder, baking soda, salt, coriander, garam masala, ginger, and onion powder in a large bowl and stir with a whisk.

After the potatoes are soft, drain them and mash them until all lumps are gone. Measure 1 cup of the mashed potatoes into a medium bowl and thoroughly mix with the plant milk, oil, sugar, lemon juice, and garlic. Pour the wet mixture into the flour mixture and stir just until blended. Fold in the peas, cashews, and raisins.

Preheat the waffle iron according to the manufacturer's directions. Spray both grids with oil. Pour or ladle the batter into the center of the iron, covering no more than two-thirds of the iron's surface for the first waffle. Adjust the amount as needed for subsequent waffles. Bake each waffle for 4 to 5 minutes, or until it can be removed easily.

Sesame Waffles

Makes 4 (7 in. or 18 cm) round Belgian waffles

Remember the secret phrase for entry to the waffle party: "Open, iron with sesame waffle!" A bit on the sweeter side of savory, these are light and slightly crispy, with additional texture from the seeds. Warm maple syrup or Lemon-Ginger Drizzle (page 130) creates a delicious combination.

3/4 cup (109 g) all-purpose flour
3/4 cup (105 g) whole wheat flour
2 teaspoons baking powder
1 teaspoon baking soda
1 1/4 teaspoons salt
1/2 cup (70 g) raw hulled sesame seeds (see note)
1 1/2 cups plus 2 tablespoons (380 ml) soy milk or other plant milk
1/2 cup (100 g) sugar
1/2 cup (128 g) tahini (sesame seed butter)
1/4 cup (60 ml) canola or other vegetable oil
2 tablespoons ground flaxseed
2 tablespoons lemon juice

Combine the all-purpose flour, whole wheat flour, baking powder, baking soda, salt, and sesame seeds in a large bowl and stir with a whisk. Thoroughly mix the plant milk, sugar, tahini, oil, flaxseed, and lemon juice in a medium bowl. Pour the wet mixture into the flour mixture and stir just until blended.

Preheat the waffle iron according to the manufacturer's directions. Spray both grids generously with oil. Pour or ladle the batter into the center of the iron, covering no more than two-thirds of the iron's surface for the first waffle. Adjust the amount as needed for subsequent waffles. Bake each waffle for 3 to 4 minutes, or until it can be removed easily.

Note: Hulled (decorticated) sesame seeds have a clean and nutty flavor compared to whole seeds, which have a more complex but slightly bitter flavor. Starting with toasted seeds will give you a stronger toasted flavor than starting with raw seeds. You may need to experiment to see which you prefer.

Refried Bean, Rice, & Cornmeal Waffles (GF)

Makes 5 (7 in. or 18 cm) round Belgian waffles

These are a bit lighter and crispier than the Refried Bean and Cornmeal Waffles (page 98). Salsa, guacamole, vegan sour cream, and vegan cheese remain the perfect match for the subtle citrus and warm spices.

> 1 1/4 cups (198 g) brown rice flour
> 1/2 cup (64 g) tapioca flour
> 3/4 cup (128 g) cornmeal
> 2 teaspoons baking powder
> 1 teaspoon baking soda
> 1 teaspoon salt (see note)
> 1 3/4 teaspoons xanthan gum powder
> 1 3/4 teaspoons ground cumin
> 1 teaspoon onion powder
> 1/8 teaspoon ground cayenne
> 1 1/2 cups (350 ml) soy milk or other plant milk
> 1 can (15 oz./425 g) refried black beans, drained and rinsed
> 1/4 cup plus 2 tablespoons (90 ml) canola or other vegetable oil
> 3 tablespoons lime juice
> 3 tablespoons sugar

Combine the rice flour, tapioca flour, cornmeal, baking powder, baking soda, salt, xanthan gum powder, cumin, onion powder, and cayenne in a large bowl and stir with a whisk. Thoroughly mix the plant milk, beans, oil, lime juice, and sugar in a medium bowl. Pour the wet mixture into the flour mixture and stir until well blended. Let stand for 3 to 5 minutes, while preheating the waffle iron according to the manufacturer's directions.

Stir the batter another 5 to 10 strokes, to get rid of any remaining rice flour clumps. Spray both grids with oil. Pour or ladle the batter into the center of the iron, covering no more than two-thirds of the iron's surface for the first waffle. Adjust the amount as needed for subsequent waffles. Bake each waffle for 4 to 6 minutes, or until it can be removed easily.

Note: Reduce the salt to 3/4 teaspoon or less if beans are heavily salted.

Mucho Molassesey Vegan Power Waffles (GF)

Makes 4 (7 in. or 18 cm) round Belgian waffles

Great for the physically active waffler, these pack more potassium and protein than the average waffle. Their strong molasses flavor is not for the faint of heart, especially if blackstrap molasses is used. Top with chocolate or carob chips, or Maple Syrup Supreme (page 128).

> 1 3/4 cups (277 g) brown rice flour
> 1/2 cup (64 g) tapioca flour
> 1/2 cup (62 g) hemp powder (ground hempseed)
> 2 teaspoons baking powder
> 1 teaspoon baking soda
> 1 teaspoon salt
> 1 teaspoon xanthan gum powder
> 1/2 teaspoon ground cinnamon (optional)
> 2 ripe medium bananas (2/3 cup, 160 ml, or 180 g peeled and mashed)
> 2 1/4 cups (530 ml) soy milk or other plant milk
> 1/4 cup plus 2 tablespoons (90 ml) canola or other vegetable oil
> 1/4 cup plus 2 tablespoons (90 ml) molasses
> 1 teaspoon vanilla extract

Combine the rice flour, tapioca flour, hemp powder, baking powder, baking soda, salt, xanthan gum powder, and cinnamon in a large bowl and stir with a whisk. Mash the bananas in a medium bowl, and thoroughly mix with the plant milk, oil, molasses, and vanilla extract. Pour the wet mixture into the flour mixture and stir until well blended.

Let stand for 3 to 5 minutes, while preheating the waffle iron according to the manufacturer's directions.

Stir the batter another 5 to 10 strokes, to get rid of any remaining rice flour clumps. Spray both grids of the waffle iron generously with oil. Pour or ladle the batter into the center of the iron, covering no more than two-thirds of the iron's surface for the first waffle. Adjust the amount as needed for subsequent waffles. Bake each waffle for 4 to 5 minutes, or until it can be removed easily.

Gluten-Free Umami Mama Waffles (GF)

Makes 3 to 4 (7 in. or 18 cm) round Belgian Waffles

Compared to the wheat flour version (page 100), these delectable pizza-like treats are a bit crispier. Savor them as they are or enjoy with the Savory Cashew-Mushroom Sauce (page 151). Because the batter needs time to ferment, begin at least 3 hours in advance of baking or 1 1/2 hours in advance if you are using quick-rise yeast.

1 1/4 teaspoons active dry yeast

1 1/2 cups (350 ml) warm water (see "Yeasted Waffle Tips," page 25)

1 1/2 cups plus 3 tablespoons (267 g) brown rice flour

1/2 cup plus 1 tablespoon (72 g) tapioca flour

3/4 teaspoon salt

1/3 cup (56 g) pitted and finely chopped Kalamata olives

1/3 cup (70 g) finely chopped sun-dried tomatoes, preserved in olive oil or rehydrated

1/2 cup plus 1 tablespoon (135 ml) soy milk or other plant milk

1/4 cup (60 ml) olive or other vegetable oil

3 tablespoons nutritional yeast flakes

1 tablespoon plus 1 teaspoon light or chickpea miso

1/4 cup (22 g) ground flaxseed

1 tablespoon sugar

2 medium cloves garlic, crushed

1 teaspoon baking powder

1 teaspoon dried basil

1 teaspoon onion powder

1 teaspoon dried oregano

1/8 teaspoon ground cayenne (optional)

Dissolve the yeast in the water in a large non-metal bowl. Let stand for 5 minutes. Stir in the rice flour, tapioca flour, and salt until well blended. Cover the bowl and place it in a warm location so the flour mixture can ferment—for at least 3 hours, or 1 1/2 hours if using quick-rise yeast (see "Yeasted Waffle Tips," page 23). Because this is a gluten-free mixture, it may expand only slightly, but the process will still add some flavor and texture.

After the flour mixture has fermented, chop the olives and sun-dried tomatoes, and set aside. Combine the plant milk, oil, nutritional yeast, miso, flaxseed, sugar, garlic, baking powder, basil, onion powder, oregano, and cayenne in a medium bowl. Mix thoroughly, breaking up any clumps of miso. Pour into the fermented flour mixture and stir until well blended. Fold in the olives and sun-dried tomatoes.

Let stand for 15 minutes, while preheating the waffle iron according to the manufacturer's directions.

Spray both grids of the waffle iron generously with oil—this is especially important for gluten-free recipes with flaxseed, even if your iron is "non-stick." Pour or ladle the batter into the center of the iron, covering no more than two-thirds of the iron's surface for the first waffle. Adjust the amount as needed for subsequent waffles. Bake each waffle for 4 to 6 minutes, or until it can be removed easily.

Gluten-Free Kale-idoscopic Waffles (GF)

Makes 4 (7 in. or 18 cm) round Belgian waffles

A peanutty-spicy blend accents bits of deliciously nutritious green kale in this gluten-free version of the original (page 107). Top with Simple Piña Colada-ish Topping (page 134), bits of juicy pineapple, or slices of sautéed onion.

> 3 cups (94 g) packed fresh kale, leaf stems removed before measuring, finely chopped (any variety, see note)
> 1 3/4 cups plus 2 tablespoons (440 ml) soy milk or other plant milk
> 1/2 cup (128 g) smooth peanut butter (see note)
> 3 tablespoons soy sauce
> 3 tablespoons sugar
> 1/4 cup (22 g) ground flaxseed
> 1 tablespoon cider vinegar
> 2 medium cloves garlic, crushed
> 1 1/2 cups (237 g) rice flour
> 1/2 cup (64 g) tapioca flour
> 2 teaspoons baking powder
> 1/2 teaspoon baking soda
> 1 1/2 teaspoons onion powder
> 1/8 teaspoon ground cayenne (optional)

Chop the kale and set aside. Thoroughly mix the plant milk, peanut butter, soy sauce, sugar, ground flaxseed, vinegar, and garlic in a medium bowl. Break up any clumps of peanut butter. Combine the rice flour, tapioca flour, baking powder, baking soda, onion powder, and cayenne in a large bowl and stir with a whisk. Pour the wet mixture into the flour mixture and stir until well blended. Fold in the kale.

Let stand for 3 to 4 minutes, while preheating the waffle iron according to the manufacturer's directions.

Spray both grids of the waffle iron with oil—this is especially important for gluten-free recipes with flaxseed, even if your iron is "non-stick." Pour or ladle the batter into the center of the iron, covering no more than two-thirds of the iron's surface for the first waffle. Adjust the amount as needed for subsequent waffles. Before closing the iron, manually spread the batter out slightly with the ladle or a spatula if needed so the kale doesn't all get stuck near the center. Bake each waffle for 4 to 5 minutes, or until it can be removed easily.

Notes: The kale should be chopped into pieces no larger than your thumbnail. If it is not chopped finely enough, the waffles will be more likely to separate in the middle upon opening the iron.

If you're using peanut butter that has been refrigerated, warming it in the microwave may make it easier to mix into the batter.

Flavory-Sweet Waffle Toppings

You may often be in the mood for a waffle with a warm drizzle of maple syrup or some fresh slices of colorful fruit on top. There's certainly nothing wrong with that. However, as you expand your waffle horizons, you may crave more complexity. While some of the following toppings are designed to accompany specific waffles, or include specific pairing suggestions, feel free to try whatever topping-waffle combinations sound tasty to you. Perhaps even experiment with some of them on vegan ice cream or cake. You may discover a previously unknown flavor combination!

Dark Chocolate Syrup & Variations

Makes about 3/4 cup (180 ml)

This has a deeper and more bittersweet chocolate flavor than most store-bought chocolate syrups. It complements strawberries and other fresh fruit toppings, as well as vegan ice cream. Enjoy with PBMax Waffles (page 69) or Cider-Pecan Waffles (page 70).

1/2 cup (100 g) sugar
1/4 cup plus 1 tablespoon (28 g) cocoa powder
1/4 cup (56 g) vegan butter
1/4 cup (60 ml) soy milk or other plant milk
1 teaspoon vanilla extract

Combine all the ingredients except the vanilla extract in a small saucepan. Stir briskly and constantly over medium heat until half a minute after it begins to boil. Continue to scrape the bottom to incorporate any dry cocoa and keep it from burning. Immediately remove from heat and stir in the vanilla extract.

Dark Chocolate Amaretto Syrup: Add 2 or 3 tablespoons of amaretto after turning off heat.

Dark Chocolate Orangalicious Syrup: Add 1 teaspoon of orange extract after turning off heat.

Dark Chocolate Peebee Syrup: Add 1/4 cup (64 g) smooth or chunky peanut butter before heating. Other nut butters, such as cashew or almond, can also provide an extra-rich flavor.

South of the Border Dark Chocolate Syrup: Add 1 teaspoon of ground cinnamon and 1/8 teaspoon of ground cayenne before heating.

Crazeee Carob Syrup

Makes about 3/4 cup (180 ml)

This provides a complex dimension of richness different from that of the Dark Chocolate Syrup (page 125). Drizzle atop Mucho Molassesey Vegan Power Waffles (page 118).

> **1/3 cup (40 g) toasted carob powder**
> **1/3 cup (67 g) sugar**
> **1/4 cup (56 g) vegan butter**
> **1/4 cup (60 ml) soy milk or other plant milk**
> **1 teaspoon vanilla extract**

Combine all the ingredients except the vanilla extract in a small saucepan. Stir briskly and constantly over medium heat until half a minute after it begins to boil. Immediately remove from heat and stir in the vanilla extract.

Note: For variation ideas, see variations for Dark Chocolate Syrup (page 125).

Banana-Maple-Nut Syrup

Makes 3/4 cup (180 ml)

This textured, salty-sweet accompaniment meshes well with the Banana-Fofana-Walnut Waffles (page 99) or the Banana-Blueberry-Teff Waffles (page 79).

> **1 ripe medium banana (1/3 cup, 80 ml, or 90 g peeled and mashed)**
> **1/4 cup (60 ml) maple syrup**
> **1/4 cup (30 g) finely chopped pecans or walnuts**
> **1/8 teaspoon salt (reduce or omit if nuts are already salted)**

Mash the banana in a small saucepan, and mix with the maple syrup, nuts, and salt. Stir constantly over medium heat, just until warm.

Cocoa or Carob Agave Nectar

Makes about 1 cup (240 ml)

This decadent sauce takes the Dark Chocolate Syrup (page 125) and Crazeee Carob Syrup (page 126) in yet another direction with molasses overtones. Pour over Dark Chocolate Cake Waffles (page 67) or Cashew-Carob-Molasses Waffles (page 84) and vegan ice cream for a deep, dark, delicious dessert.

> 1/2 cup (120 ml) agave nectar
> 1/4 cup plus 1 tablespoon (28 g) cocoa powder
> 1/4 cup plus 1 tablespoon (75 ml) molasses
> 1/4 cup (56 g) vegan butter
> 1 teaspoon vanilla extract

Combine all the ingredients except the vanilla extract in a small saucepan. Stir constantly over medium heat just until it begins to boil, the vegan butter is entirely melted, and the cocoa and sugar are well dissolved. Immediately remove from heat and stir in the vanilla extract.

Carob Agave Nectar: Replace the cocoa powder with 1/4 cup plus 2 tablespoons (45 g) of toasted carob powder.

Espresso-Maple-Walnut Syrup

Makes 1 cup (240 ml)

Nuts, maple, and additional espresso zing enhance the Espresso-Key Lime Waffles (page 75) or the Banana-Fofana-Walnut Waffles (page 99).

1/4 cup (30 g) finely chopped walnuts
1 teaspoon instant espresso granules
2 tablespoons hot water
1/4 cup (60 ml) maple syrup
1/4 cup (60 ml) plain or vanilla dairy-free yogurt
1 tablespoon brown sugar
1 tablespoon vegan butter
1/8 teaspoon salt

Chop the walnuts and set aside. Dissolve the espresso granules in the hot water in a small saucepan. (The hottest water from the tap should work.) Add the maple syrup, dairy-free yogurt, brown sugar, vegan butter, salt, and walnuts. Stir constantly over medium heat until the vegan butter is melted.

Maple Syrup Supreme

Makes 1 1/4 cups (300 ml)

If you love maple syrup and desire a fuller and more complex flavor, this is sure to please. Generously ladle onto the Pass the Buckwheat-Oat Waffles (page 45) or the Crispy Maple-Cashew Waffles (page 80).

3/4 cup (180 ml) maple syrup
1/4 cup (56 g) vegan butter
1/4 cup (60 ml) molasses

Combine all the ingredients in a small saucepan. Stir constantly over medium heat until the vegan butter is melted and the mixture just begins to boil.

Coco Kah-banana Syrup

Makes 1 to 1 1/4 cups (240 to 300 ml)

For coffee flavor with a tropical twist, place this atop the Espresso-Key Lime Waffles (page 75). It also plays well with the Dark Chocolate Cake Waffles (page 67).

> **1 ripe medium banana (1/3 cup, 80 ml, or 90 g peeled and mashed)**
> **1/2 cup (120 ml) full-fat coconut milk**
> **1/4 cup (60 ml) Kahlua or other coffee-flavored liqueur (see note for alcohol-free version)**
> **1/4 cup (50 g) sugar**

Mash the banana in a small bowl, and mix with the coconut milk, Kahlua, and sugar until the sugar is dissolved.

Note: For an alcohol-free version, omit liqueur, add 2 teaspoons instant coffee granules dissolved in 1/4 cup (60 ml) of warm water, and increase sugar by 1 tablespoon.

Very Coconutty Syrup

Makes about 1 cup (240 ml)

Coconutty is oh-so-nutty. This blend embellishes the Mango-Chili Waffles (page 76) or adds a super coconuttiness to the Coconut-Date Waffles (page 81).

> 1/4 cup (13 g) finely shredded unsweetened coconut (macaroon style)
> 1/4 cup (60 ml) full-fat coconut milk
> 1/4 cup (60 ml) plain or vanilla dairy-free yogurt (see note)
> 1/4 cup (50 g) sugar
> 2 tablespoons water
> 1/2 teaspoon vanilla extract

Combine all the ingredients in a small bowl and mix until the sugar is dissolved.

Note: If you'd like the topping even sweeter and even more coconutty, omit the dairy-free yogurt. This will yield about 3/4 cup (180 ml).

Lemon-Ginger Drizzle

Makes 1 1/4 cups (300 ml)

Tart and sweet with the added warmth of ginger, this sauce provides a flavorful accent to the Carrot-Ginger-Sage Waffles (page 94) or the Generously Ginger-Lemon-Chocolate Waffles (page 66).

> 1/2 cup (112 g) vegan butter
> 1/2 cup (120 ml) soy milk or other plant milk
> 1/2 cup (100 g) sugar
> 1 tablespoon plus 2 teaspoons lemon juice
> 2 1/2 teaspoons ground ginger

Combine all the ingredients in a small saucepan. Stir constantly over medium heat, continuing for half a minute after the mixture begins to boil.

Raspberry-Avocado Cream

Makes about 1 cup (240 ml)

A striking color combination adds visual appeal, and the blend tastes delicious atop the Chocolate-Raspberry Cheesecakey Waffles (page 72) or the Dark Chocolate Cake Waffles (page 67).

> **1 ripe medium avocado (163 g without peel or pit)**
> **1/4 cup (50 g) sugar**
> **2 teaspoons lemon juice**
> **1/2 teaspoon vanilla extract**
> **3/4 cup to 1 cup (98 g to 130 g) raspberries**

Scoop out the avocado. Place the avocado, sugar, lemon juice, and vanilla extract in a food processor and process until smooth and creamy. Place a few spoonfuls atop a waffle and embellish with raspberries.

If you don't have a food processor, mash the avocado in a medium bowl until all lumps are gone. Add the sugar, lemon juice, and vanilla extract, and mix until the sugar is dissolved.

Cinnamon Cream Cheese

Makes 1 cup (240 ml)

If you're craving cinnamon buns, spread some of this creamy delight onto the Original Cinnamon-Raisin Waffles (page 63) or the Yeast-Raised Cinnamon-Raisin Waffles (page 64).

    1/3 cup (37 g) raw cashews
    1/4 cup (60 ml) maple syrup
    1 tablespoon lemon juice
    6 oz. (170 g) crumbled firm silken tofu (about 2/3 cup or 160 ml)
    1/2 teaspoon ground cinnamon
    1/4 teaspoon salt

Place the cashews, maple syrup, and lemon juice in a blender, and process for several minutes until the cashews are liquefied and the mixture is smooth and creamy. Stop as necessary to scrape down the sides of the blender bowl. Add the tofu, cinnamon, and salt, and blend until the mixture is smooth again.

Creamy Maple-Chai Dream Sauce

Makes about 1 cup (240 ml)

The spicy warmth of this topping enhances the Sinful Cheesecakey Waffles (page 71) or the Dark Chocolate Cake Waffles (page 67).

> 6 oz. (170 g) crumbled soft or firm silken tofu
>   (about 2/3 cup or 160 ml)
> 1/3 cup (80 ml) maple syrup
> 1/2 teaspoon vanilla extract
> 1/4 teaspoon ground cinnamon
> 1/4 teaspoon ground ginger
> 1/8 teaspoon ground cardamom
> 1/8 teaspoon ground clove
> 1/8 teaspoon ground or grated nutmeg

Place all ingredients in a blender and process until smooth and creamy. Stop as necessary to scrape down the sides of the blender bowl.

Note: For a "buttery" overtone, add 1/8 teaspoon of salt before blending.

Creamy Spiced Apple Pie Sauce

Makes 3/4 cup (180 ml)

This sweet and tart topping is much quicker to make than an apple pie, and is delicious hot or cold. For a taste reminiscent of a country dessert, spoon onto some Crunchy Steel City Waffles (page 55).

> **1/2 cup (120 ml) applesauce**
> **1/4 cup (60 ml) vanilla dairy-free yogurt**
> **1 tablespoon vegan butter**
> **1 to 2 teaspoons sugar (optional)**
> **1/4 teaspoon ground cinnamon**
> **1/8 teaspoon allspice**
> **1/8 teaspoon ground or grated nutmeg**

Combine all the ingredients in a small saucepan. Stir constantly over medium heat just until the vegan butter is melted and the sugar is dissolved.

Simple Piña Colada-ish Topping

Makes about 1 cup (240 ml)

"Excuse me, does this beach have an outlet for a waffle iron?" This refreshing tropical treat goes nicely with the Kale-idoscopic Waffles (page 107), if you desire something adventurous.

> **3/4 cup (183 g) crushed pineapple or pineapple bits with juice**
> **1/4 cup plus 2 tablespoons (90 ml) full-fat coconut milk**
> **1 teaspoon sugar**
> **1/2 teaspoon vanilla extract**

Fill a measuring cup to the 3/4 cup mark with pineapple, adding pineapple juice to the cup so that all spaces between the pineapple are filled with juice up to the 3/4 cup mark. Combine all the ingredients in a small bowl and mix until the sugar is dissolved.

Amazing Amaretto Sauce

Makes about 3/4 cup (180 ml)

This simple but elegant syrup brings additional warmth and sweetness to the Almond-Amaranth Waffles (page 74) or the Sinful Cheesecakey Waffles (page 71).

> 1/4 cup (60 ml) amaretto liqueur (see note for alcohol-free version)
> 1/4 cup (56 g) vegan butter
> 1/4 cup (60 ml) plain or vanilla dairy-free yogurt
> 1/4 cup (50 g) sugar

Combine all the ingredients in a small saucepan. Stir constantly over medium heat just until the vegan butter is melted and the sugar is dissolved.

Note: For an alcohol-free version, omit liqueur and add 1/4 cup plant milk, 1 teaspoon almond extract, and 1 more tablespoon of sugar.

Carob Halvah Spread

Makes 1 cup (240 ml)

This thick and quick topping adds richness to a range of waffles. Put a bit on the Cashew-Carob-Molasses Waffles (page 84) for a supercharged carob experience.

> 1/2 cup (120 ml) agave nectar
> 1/2 cup (128 g) tahini (sesame seed butter)
> 2 tablespoons toasted carob powder

Combine all the ingredients in a small bowl and mix until well blended. Serve at room temperature, warm slightly for a thinner consistency, or chill for a very thick consistency.

Cinnamon-Carob Halvah Spread: Add 1 1/2 teaspoons of ground cinnamon.

Mexican Chocolate Ice Cream

Makes 3 3/4 cups (880 ml)

The coolness of ice cream and warmth of cayenne create a smooth, palatable paradox. For a really richly spiced chocolate delight, spoon a few scoops between quarters of Chai Spice Waffles (page 73).

> 1 can (14 oz./400 ml) full-fat coconut milk
> 1 1/4 cups (300 ml) soy milk or other plant milk
> 3/4 cup to 1 cup (150 g to 200 g) sugar
> 1/2 cup (44 g) cocoa powder
> 3 tablespoons canola or other neutrally flavored vegetable oil
> 2 teaspoons vanilla extract (see note)
> 1 1/4 teaspoons ground cinnamon
> 1/8 teaspoon ground cayenne
> 1/8 teaspoon salt
> 1/8 teaspoon xanthan gum powder (optional, to thicken slightly)

Combine all the ingredients in a blender and process for 2 to 3 minutes, or until the mixture is smooth and creamy. Stop midway to taste the mixture, and increase the sugar to the desired sweetness if necessary. Place the mixture in the freezer in a freezer-safe container for 45 to 60 minutes, or in the refrigerator for 90 minutes, to bring the temperature down.

Pour the mixture into an ice cream maker and freeze according to the manufacturer's directions. Enjoy immediately or place in the freezer for an hour for a harder consistency. If the ice cream has been in the freezer overnight or longer, allow it to soften at room temperature for 5 to 10 minutes before serving.

Note: Because alcohol may impede freezing, use alcohol-free extract if possible.

Mango-Vanilla Ice Cream

Makes 5 cups (1.2 L)

This multiplies the mango factor of the Mango-Chili Waffles (page 76) or adds a tropical twist to the Sinful Cheesecakey Waffles (page 71).

> 2 ripe finely chopped and chilled mangoes (between 1 1/2 and 2 cups, 340 g, see note)
> 3 cups (700 ml) soy milk or other plant milk
> 3/4 cup to 1 cup (150 g to 200 g) sugar
> 3 tablespoons canola or other neutrally flavored vegetable oil
> 1 tablespoon plus 1 teaspoon vanilla extract (see note)
> 1/8 teaspoon xanthan gum powder (optional, to thicken slightly)

Chop the mangoes and place them in the refrigerator to chill. Combine the plant milk, sugar, oil, vanilla extract, and xanthan gum powder in a blender and process for 2 to 3 minutes, or until the mixture is smooth and creamy. Stop midway to taste the mixture, and increase the sugar to the desired sweetness if necessary. Place the mixture in the freezer in a freezer-safe container for 45 to 60 minutes, or in the refrigerator for at least 90 minutes, to bring the temperature down.

Pour the mixture into an ice cream maker and freeze according to the manufacturer's directions. Fold in the chopped mangoes. Enjoy immediately or place in the freezer for an hour for a harder consistency. If the ice cream has been in the freezer overnight or longer, allow it to soften at room temperature for 5 to 10 minutes before serving.

Note: If you don't have fresh mangoes, you may substitute an equal amount of frozen mango. You may, of course, need to thaw it a bit before chopping.

Note: Because alcohol may impede freezing, use alcohol-free extract if possible.

Mango-Vanilla-Coconut Ice Cream: Add 1 can (14 oz./400 ml) full-fat coconut milk and reduce the plant milk to 1 1/4 cups (300 ml).

Basil-Orange Ice Cream

Makes 3 3/4 cups (880 ml)

This chilly confection is particularly refreshing for summertime waffles, especially if fresh basil is growing in the garden. For orange-basil abundance, pair with the Orange-Basil-Cornmeal Waffles (page 96).

> **1 can (14 oz./400 ml) full-fat coconut milk**
> **1 1/4 cups (300 ml) soy milk or other plant milk**
> **3/4 cup to 1 cup (150 g to 200 g) sugar**
> **1/2 cup (13 g) packed fresh basil leaves**
> **3 tablespoons canola or other neutrally flavored vegetable oil**
> **1 1/4 teaspoons orange extract (see note)**
> **1 teaspoon vanilla extract (see note)**
> **1/8 teaspoon xanthan gum powder (optional, to thicken slightly)**

Combine all the ingredients in a blender and process for 2 to 3 minutes, or until the mixture is smooth and the basil leaves are very finely chopped. Stop midway to taste the mixture, and increase the sugar to the desired sweetness if necessary. Place the mixture in the freezer in a freezer-safe container for 45 to 60 minutes, or in the refrigerator for at least 90 minutes, to bring the temperature down.

Pour the mixture into an ice cream maker and freeze according to the manufacturer's directions. Enjoy immediately or place in the freezer for an hour for a harder consistency. If the ice cream has been in the freezer overnight or longer, allow it to soften at room temperature for 5 to 10 minutes before serving.

Note: Because alcohol may impede freezing, use alcohol-free extract if possible.

Peanut Butter-Carob Fudge Spread

Makes 2/3 cup (160 ml)

This thick, dark, tongue-tantalizing topping blends well with fresh banana slices. Top your favorite neutral waffle with delicious goodness. Or, for an over-the-top rich treat, pair with Dark Chocolate Cake Waffles (page 67), PBMax Waffles (page 69), or Cashew-Carob-Molasses Waffles (page 84).

1/4 cup (30 g) toasted carob powder
1/4 cup (64 g) smooth peanut butter
1/4 cup (60 ml) maple syrup
2 tablespoons vegan butter
1/2 teaspoon vanilla extract

Place all ingredients except vanilla in a small saucepan. Stir constantly over low to medium heat until the vegan butter is fully melted and clumps are gone. Use a whisk if necessary. Remove from heat and stir in vanilla. Serve warm.

Blueberry Spice Syrup

Makes about 1 3/4 cups (410 ml)

In this deliciously dark, sweet, slightly tart vegan waffle syrup, blueberries play alongside subtle spices. It was inspired by a few toppings brought to past waffle parties. Drizzle atop Textured Rice Waffles (page 52), baked so they're slightly crispy.

>   1 cup (240 ml) maple syrup
>   1 cup (148 g) blueberries
>   2 tablespoons lemon juice
>   2 tablespoons vegan butter
>   1 tablespoon molasses
>   1/2 teaspoon cinnamon
>   1/4 teaspoon ginger powder

Combine all ingredients in a small saucepan or microwave safe bowl. Heat over medium heat, stirring constantly until the vegan butter is melted and blueberries are heated through. Or, heat in microwave until same result is achieved, removing every 45 seconds or so to stir and check the temperature.

Dark Chocolate-Ginger Mousse

Makes about 2 2/3 cups (630 ml), excluding banana and nuts on top

Dark chocolate plays with a fresh ginger tingle and banana overtones in this decadent, creamy vegan waffle topping. Dress up some Gluten-Free Naked Vegan Waffles (page 49) or Dark Chocolate Cake Waffles (page 67).

12 oz. (340 g) crumbled firm silken tofu (about 1 1/3 cups or 320 ml)
1/2 cup plus 2 tablespoons (70 g) raw cashews, divided
1/2 cup (44 g) cocoa powder
1/2 cup plus 2 tablespoons (125 g) sugar
2 ripe medium bananas, divided (one to be blended into mousse, one to slice and decorate top of mousse)
1/4 cup (60 ml) water
2 tablespoons melted coconut oil (see note)
2 tablespoons finely grated fresh ginger (see note)
1 teaspoon vanilla extract
3/8 teaspoon salt

Put all ingredients, except for 2 tablespoons of the cashews and one of the bananas, into a powerful blender (see note). Blend until smooth and creamy, stopping to scrape down the sides if necessary. Refrigerate for at least 3 hours, or until chilled and slightly thickened.

Shortly before serving, slice the second banana. Top the mousse with the sliced banana and the remaining 2 tablespoons of cashews.

Notes: If you use another vegetable oil, the mousse may not thicken as much.

If you don't eat ginger often, start with just 1 tablespoon of ginger and add more if needed. A trick for easier ginger grating: Store pieces of ginger root in a sealed bag in the freezer. Whenever you need some, grate it while still frozen on the fine side of a metal grater. Peeling before grating is optional.

If the mix is too thick for your blender, add more melted oil or water 1 tablespoon at a time to thin. Or, mix in a food processor and then transfer to the blender to process until smooth, 1 cup (240 ml) at a time.

Sweet Star Anise Syrup

Makes about 1 cup (240 ml)

This waffle syrup is quite sweet, with a hint of vanilla to accompany the anise. It's best served warm, but as it cools it thickens and forms a glaze, making the waffle reminiscent of a sweet doughnut. It was inspired by a childhood ritual of making rock candy in a variety of flavors including anise. That flavor is one of my dad's favorites, and I also enjoy it. Drizzle over Yeast-Raised Waffles (page 43).

3/4 cup (150 g) sugar
1/4 cup plus 2 tablespoons (84 g) vegan butter
3 tablespoons water
1 1/2 teaspoons ground star anise (about 3 stars of anise), or 1/2
    teaspoon anise extract (see note)
3/4 teaspoon vanilla

Grind 3 stars of anise in a coffee or spice grinder, as finely as possible (see note). Combine the sugar, vegan butter, water, and anise in a small saucepan. Heat over medium heat, stirring constantly, until the vegan butter is fully melted. Reduce heat to simmer and stir constantly for 5 minutes. Remove from heat and add vanilla.

Note: The syrup may have occasional tiny pieces of anise, even after the cooking softens it. I found these almost unnoticeable after the syrup was drizzled on a waffle. However, if you want a completely smooth syrup, substitute liquid extract for the fresh ground anise. Start with 1/2 teaspoon of anise extract, added after heating the rest of the mixture. Increase in 1/8 teaspoon increments until the anise flavor is the desired strength.

Coconut Ecstasy Spread

Makes about 1 cup (240 ml)

For one of the waffle parties, I needed a last-minute topping. Spread onto some Textured Rice Waffles (page 52) for extra ecstasy, or just eat huge globs off a spoon when nobody's looking.

> 1/2 cup (112 g) coconut manna or coconut butter, at room temperature
> 3 tablespoons vegan butter, at room temperature
> 2 tablespoons agave nectar
> 1/3 cup (57 g) vegan chocolate chips, divided
> 1/3 cup (47 g) dried cranberries, divided

Soften the coconut manna by placing the jar in a bowl of hot or warm water if necessary, to make it stirrable. Soften the vegan butter in the microwave if necessary, just until it's stirrable. Mix the coconut manna, vegan butter, and agave nectar in a small bowl until well blended. Fold in all but 1 tablespoon of the chocolate chips, and all but 1 tablespoon of the cranberries. Stir until evenly distributed. Sprinkle the remaining chocolate chips and cranberries on top.

Chocolate-Pumpkin Mousse

Makes about 4 cups (950 ml)

This tongue tantalizer is a wonderful way to top off a fall or winter day. For the epitome of sweet pumpkin, spice, and chocolate so nice, spoon generously onto Sweet Yeast-Raised Waffles (page 44) or Mapley Waffles (page 50).

3/4 cup (128 g) vegan chocolate chips, melted
1/4 cup (56 g) vegan butter, softened
12 oz. (340 g) crumbled firm silken tofu (about 1 1/3 cups or 320 ml)
1 can (15 oz./425 g) pureed pumpkin
1/4 cup (46 g) brown sugar
3 tablespoons rum (optional)
2 tablespoons molasses
1 teaspoon vanilla extract
1/2 teaspoon cinnamon
1/4 teaspoon ground ginger
1/8 teaspoon ground nutmeg or mace

Combine the chocolate chips and vegan butter in a small bowl, and heat in the microwave at 45- to 60-second intervals just until the chocolate is melted and most lumps can be stirred out. (Time may need to be adjusted depending upon your microwave's power.) Alternately, melt the mixture in a small saucepan over low to medium heat, heating just until the chocolate has melted and stirring constantly to avoid burning the chocolate.

Combine the softened chocolate chips and vegan butter with all other ingredients in a blender, and process until smooth. This is a thick mixture, so you may need to stop the blender several times to push the unmixed portion down toward the blades with a large spoon or spatula. If you sense you're maxing out your blender's power and size capacity, divide the mixture into two portions, blend them separately until smooth, and then blend them back together at the end. Or, mix in a food processor and then transfer to the blender to process until smooth. Refrigerate for at least an hour before serving to thicken.

Note: To make it extra fancy, top with finely chopped candied ginger and finely chopped chocolate chips.

Peanut Butter Fluff

Makes 1 3/4 cups (410 ml)

This creamy palate pleaser will accompany any neutral waffle. For a classic flavor combo, serve with Dark Chocolate Cake Waffles (page 67). If you're really wild about peanut butter, spoon onto some PBMax Waffles (page 69).

> 6 oz. (170 g) crumbled firm silken tofu (about 2/3 cup or 160 ml)
> 3/4 cup (90 g) vegan confectioner's sugar
> 3/4 cup (192 g) smooth peanut butter
> 1/4 cup (56 g) vegan butter, softened but not melted
> 1 tablespoon molasses
> 2 teaspoons vanilla extract

Combine all ingredients in a medium bowl and stir until everything is well incorporated. The mixture will still be a bit lumpy. Cover and refrigerate for at least 2 hours, or until chilled. Shortly before serving, beat at medium to high speed with a powered hand mixer for 3 to 5 minutes, or until smooth and fluffy.

Note: If you don't have a hand mixer, a blender will work, but the topping may have a denser consistency.

Kicky Waffle Syrup

Makes 1 1/4 cups (300 ml)

Add a warm, sweet, and spicy kick to your favorite vegan waffles with this delicious topping. Accompany with dairy-free vanilla ice cream, dried cranberries, and walnuts, if you like. It also works well as an oatmeal mix-in.

> 1 cup (240 ml) real maple syrup
> 1/4 cup (60 ml) molasses
> 1 teaspoon cinnamon
> 1/2 teaspoon ground ginger
> 1/4 teaspoon ground nutmeg or mace
> 1/4 teaspoon salt

Combine all ingredients in a small saucepan. Stir constantly over medium heat until the spices are dissolved and syrup is desired warmth.

Peanut Butter-Coffee Waffle Topping

Makes about 1 1/4 cups (300 ml)

Thanks to a long-term vegan waffle party host for reminding me how well peanut butter goes with chocolate vegan waffles. I grew up near an ice cream shop and loved their peanut butter syrup. As a child, I spent a few hours in the kitchen trying to reverse engineer it. Years later, here it is with a twist. Drizzle over Dark Chocolate Cake Waffles (page 67). Or, for a flavor reminiscent of breakfast donuts and coffee, pair with Sweet Yeast-Raised Waffles (page 44) or Mapley Waffles (page 50).

> 1/2 cup (120 ml) hot water
> 1/2 cup (92 g) brown sugar
> 1 1/2 teaspoons instant coffee granules (see note)
> 1 cup (256 g) smooth peanut butter

Combine the hot water, brown sugar, and coffee granules in a small saucepan. Stir constantly over medium heat until the sugar and coffee granules are dissolved. Add the peanut butter and stir constantly just until evenly warm.

Notes: Reduce coffee granules to 1 teaspoon if you want just a hint of coffee flavor.

This is a thick topping. To thin, add water or plant milk 1 tablespoon at a time and continue to stir constantly over medium heat until evenly warm.

Coconut Whipped Cream

Makes about 1 3/4 cups (410 ml)

This topping is very versatile. Employ it alongside fresh fruit or Dark Chocolate Syrup (page 125), or use it as a sole topping on waffles with complex flavors. Spoon onto some Easy Coconut-Almond Waffles (page 89), Original Cinnamon-Raisin Waffles (page 63), or Yeast-Raised Cinnamon Raisin Waffles (page 64).

1 can (14 oz./400 ml) full-fat coconut milk or cream
1 tablespoon maple syrup or agave nectar (optional)
1 1/2 teaspoons vanilla extract (optional)

Refrigerate the can of coconut milk overnight or longer. Just before serving, combine all ingredients in a medium bowl. For best results, use a chilled mixing bowl. Beat at medium to high speed with a powered hand mixer for 3 to 5 minutes, or until smooth and fluffy. Spoon onto your favorite waffle ASAP, as the cream will begin to lose fluffiness as it sits and warms.

For thicker cream: When you put the can of coconut milk in the fridge, make sure the side facing down is a side you can open with your can opener. As it chills, the cream will float to the top, leaving some water at the bottom.

At preparation time, invert the can and open the end that was on the bottom. Pour off the water and set it aside. If you have coconut cream rather than coconut milk, or coconut milk with additives that prevent separation, there may be little or no liquid to pour off. Coconut milks vary in this respect, so it might take a few tries to find the brand or variety that works best for you.

If needed, break down any firm clumps of cream with a spoon, food processor, or blender before adding the other ingredients and whipping with the hand mixer. If it is too thick to whip, add back some of the poured-off liquid a tablespoon at a time.

Flavory-Savory Waffle Toppings

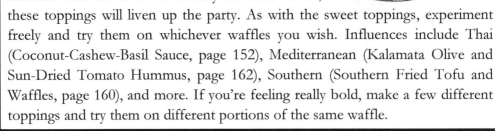

Forget the myth that only sweet toppings may go on waffles. Whether you wish to add excitement to a neutral waffle or increase the moisture and flavor of an already-flavorful waffle, these toppings will liven up the party. As with the sweet toppings, experiment freely and try them on whichever waffles you wish. Influences include Thai (Coconut-Cashew-Basil Sauce, page 152), Mediterranean (Kalamata Olive and Sun-Dried Tomato Hummus, page 162), Southern (Southern Fried Tofu and Waffles, page 160), and more. If you're feeling really bold, make a few different toppings and try them on different portions of the same waffle.

Savory Cashew-Mushroom Sauce

Makes 1 1/4 cups (300 ml)

Paired with the Umami Mama Waffles (page 100), this topping creates a richness that will satisfy cravings for pizza or other savory foods. It also meshes well with the Spanakowafflita (page 105).

    2 cups (174 g) baby portabella (brown crimini) mushrooms,
        thinly sliced
    2 green onions, finely chopped
    2 medium garlic cloves, crushed
    2 tablespoons cashew butter, unsalted
    2 tablespoons soy sauce
    3 tablespoons water, divided
    1/4 cup (60 ml) plain dairy-free yogurt

Slice the mushrooms, chop the green onions, crush the garlic, and set aside. Heat the cashew butter, soy sauce, and 1 tablespoon of the water in a medium frying pan over medium heat, stirring and scraping the pan frequently with a spatula. Continue for 2 to 3 minutes, or until the cashew butter has softened and dissolved into the soy sauce.

Combine the mushrooms, green onions, and garlic with the mixture in the pan. Sauté for another 4 to 6 minutes, turning frequently and adding 1 tablespoon of the remaining water every 2 minutes. Keep the mixture just moist enough to fry and brown slightly, so it just begins to develop a crust. Stir in the dairy-free yogurt and heat for another minute, scraping the pan frequently to avoid burning.

Coconut-Cashew-Basil Sauce

Makes about 1 cup (240 ml)

This creamy, moderately sweet, and slightly tangy sauce incorporates Thai influence and provides a twist to the Orange-Basil-Cornmeal Waffles (page 96).

3/4 cup (180 ml) full-fat coconut milk
1/4 cup (64 g) cashew butter, unsalted
2 tablespoons packed fresh basil
2 teaspoons lime juice
1 tablespoon sugar
1/8 teaspoon salt

Combine all the ingredients in a blender and process for 30 to 60 seconds, or until smooth. If you don't have a blender, manually chop the basil leaves as finely as possible, and mix all the ingredients by hand until well blended.

Cilantro-Lime Tahini Sauce

Makes 3/4 cup (180 ml)

This variation from traditional tahini sauce, which often uses lemon juice and parsley, accents the Chili-Lime Felafel Waffles (page 104) nicely.

1/2 cup (120 ml) plain dairy-free yogurt
1/4 cup (64 g) tahini (sesame seed butter)
2 tablespoons lime juice
1 tablespoon finely chopped fresh cilantro (see note)
1/4 teaspoon salt

Combine all the ingredients in a small bowl, breaking up any clumps of tahini and mixing until well blended.

Note: You may substitute 1 tablespoon of finely chopped fresh parsley for the cilantro.

You Make Miso Tangy Dipping Sauce

Makes 3/4 cup (180 ml)

Melding Italian and Asian influences, this blend heightens the savoriness of waffles including the Caramelized Onion and Garlic Waffles (page 102) and the Umami Mama Waffles (page 100).

>   1/2 cup (120 ml) olive or other vegetable oil
>   1/4 cup (60 ml) balsamic vinegar
>   1 tablespoon light or chickpea miso
>   1 1/2 teaspoons sugar (or slightly more to taste)
>   1/8 teaspoon freshly ground black pepper
>   1/16 to 1/8 teaspoon ground cayenne

Combine all the ingredients in a small bowl and stir with a whisk, breaking up any chunks of miso. Dip your favorite flavory-savory waffle into the mixture and enjoy.

Note: For added spiciness, add 2 teaspoons of dried basil and 1 teaspoon of dried oregano. Cover and place in the refrigerator for 2 hours prior to serving, allowing the flavors to blend.

Mint Raita

Makes 1 1/2 cups (350 ml)

Relatively simple so that the mint shines through, this sauce adds a refreshing accent to the Spicy Carrot-Raisin Waffles (page 95) or Some Awesome Samosa Waffles (page 114).

> 1 cup (240 ml) plain dairy-free yogurt
> 1/2 medium cucumber, peeled, seeded, and finely chopped
>   (roughly 1 cup or 133 g)
> 2 tablespoons packed fresh spearmint leaves, finely chopped
> 1 teaspoon sugar
> 1/4 teaspoon salt
> 1/16 to 1/8 teaspoon ground cayenne (optional)

Combine all the ingredients in a small bowl and stir until well blended. Cover and place in the refrigerator for 2 hours prior to serving, allowing the flavors to blend.

Black Bean-Mango Tango

Makes 2 cups (475 ml)

This sweet, tangy, and refreshing blend dances well alongside the Mango-Chili Waffles (page 76) or the Refried Bean, Rice, and Cornmeal Waffles (page 117).

 1 ripe finely chopped mango (between 3/4 and 1 cup, 170 g, see note)
 1 can (15 oz./425 g) black beans, drained and rinsed
 2 tablespoons lime juice
 2 tablespoons olive or other vegetable oil
 2 teaspoons finely chopped fresh cilantro (see note)
 3/4 teaspoon chili powder
 1/2 teaspoon paprika
 1/4 teaspoon salt

Combine all the ingredients in a small bowl and stir until evenly mixed. Cover and place in the refrigerator for 1 to 2 hours, allowing the flavors to blend. Stir again just before serving.

Note: If you don't have a fresh mango, you may substitute 1 cup of previously frozen, finely chopped mango.

Note: If cilantro's not your thing, you can omit it or substitute 2 teaspoons of finely chopped fresh parsley.

Southwestern Beans & Greens

Makes 7 to 9 cups (1.7 to 2.1 L)

This rich, chili-like dish works well as a substantive topping for larger parties or as a complete entrée for smaller gatherings. It goes especially well with the Yeast-Raised Cornmeal Chili-Dippin' Waffles (page 110). Leftovers can be frozen for future lunches.

> 1 1/2 pounds (680 g) collard greens, chopped
> 2 cups (236 g) finely chopped onion
> 1/2 cup (40 g) finely chopped baby portabella (brown crimini) mushrooms
> 2 medium cloves garlic, crushed
> 1/2 cup (120 ml) olive or other vegetable oil, divided (see note)
> 1 can (28 oz./794 g) crushed tomatoes
> 1 can (15 oz./425 g) diced tomatoes
> 2 cans (15 oz./425 g each) black beans, drained and rinsed
> 1 can (15 oz./425 g) pinto beans, drained and rinsed
> 1/2 cup (30 g) nutritional yeast flakes
> 2 tablespoons dried basil
> 2 tablespoons chili powder
> 2 tablespoons ground cumin
> 2 tablespoons molasses
> 2 tablespoons sugar
> 3/4 to 1 1/2 teaspoons salt
> 1/2 teaspoon liquid smoke (optional)
> 1/4 teaspoon freshly ground black pepper
> 1/8 teaspoon ground cayenne

Chop the collard greens into bite-sized pieces, chop the onions and mushrooms, and set aside. Combine the onion, garlic, and 2 tablespoons of the oil in a large non-aluminum saucepan. Sauté over medium heat for 5 minutes or until slightly browned, stirring every 1 or 2 minutes to avoid burning. Add the mushroom and sauté for another 3 minutes. Add the remaining 1/4 cup plus 2 tablespoons (90 ml) of oil, crushed tomatoes, diced tomatoes, black beans, pinto beans, nutritional yeast, basil, chili powder, cumin, sugar, salt, liquid smoke, black pepper, and cayenne, and stir well. When the mixture starts to boil, add the collards to the pot and stir them into the mixture. They will greatly decrease in volume as they heat. Reduce the heat to low. Simmer covered for 45 minutes, stirring every 5 to 10 minutes to prevent burning. To give the flavors more time to blend, let stand in the fridge overnight.

Note: You may reduce the total amount of oil to 1/4 cup (60 ml) if you wish.

Spicy Sloppy Tofu & Portabella

Makes 4 1/2 cups (1 L)

Suitable for a main dish, this is essentially a deluxe vegan sloppy Joe. Spoon a generous serving of this satisfyingly savory topping between 2 quarters of Yeast-Raised Waffles (page 43) to form a sloppy tofu wafflewich.

> 14 oz. (397 g) extra-firm tofu, prepared in advance
>   (see How-To, page 159)
> 1 cup (80 g) finely chopped baby portabella (brown crimini)
>   mushrooms
> 3/4 cup (89 g) finely chopped onion
> 1/2 cup (152 g) finely chopped bell pepper
> 2 medium cloves garlic, crushed
> 1/4 cup plus 2 tablespoons (90 ml) olive or other vegetable oil, divided
> 1 can (28 oz./794 g) crushed tomatoes
> 1/3 cup (80 ml) molasses
> 1/3 cup (20 g) nutritional yeast flakes
> 1/4 cup (53 g) finely chopped sun-dried tomatoes, preserved in olive
>   oil or rehydrated (optional)
> 2 tablespoons brown sugar
> 1 tablespoon dried basil
> 1 tablespoon chili powder
> 1 tablespoon cider vinegar
> 1 to 1 1/2 teaspoons salt
> 1 teaspoon dried mustard powder
> 1 teaspoon dried oregano
> 1/4 to 1/2 teaspoon liquid smoke (optional)
> 1/4 teaspoon freshly ground black pepper
> 1/8 to 1/4 teaspoon ground cayenne

After the tofu has been prepared, crumble it into small pieces, and set aside in a small bowl. Chop the mushrooms, onion, and bell pepper, and set aside.

Combine the onion, garlic, and 2 tablespoons of the oil in a large non-aluminum saucepan. Sauté over medium heat for 5 minutes or until slightly browned, stirring every minute to avoid burning. Add 2 more tablespoons of oil, the mushrooms, and bell pepper, and sauté for 5 more minutes. Reduce the heat to low, and add the remaining 2 tablespoons of oil, crushed tomatoes, molasses, nutritional yeast, sun-dried tomatoes, brown sugar, basil, chili powder, vinegar, salt, mustard powder, oregano, liquid smoke, black pepper, and cayenne. Stir until well blended.

Pour the prepared tofu into the mixture. Warm the entire mixture over medium heat, stirring every 1 to 2 minutes, just until it begins to boil. Reduce the heat to low. Simmer uncovered for 45 minutes, stirring every 5 to 10 minutes to prevent burning.

How-To: Prepare Freeze and Squeeze Tofu

Open and drain the block of tofu at least 1 day in advance, and cut widthwise into 8 slices, each roughly 1 inch (2.5 cm) thick. Seal them in a freezer-tight bag or container and place it in the freezer overnight. Then remove from the freezer and thaw. Placing the bag or container in a pot of hot water can speed the thawing process to under an hour. Press 1 or 2 thawed slices at a time between your palms, squeezing out as much of the water as you can. It should now have a spongier texture that will enable it to absorb more flavor.

Southern Fried Tofu & Waffles

Makes 2 1/3 cups (550 ml)

Based upon the popular non-vegan southern dish of fried chicken and waffles, this spicy topping plays well with the Yeast-Raised Cornmeal Chili-Dippin' Waffles (page 110) or the Tropically Tanned Naked Waffles (page 42). Drizzle with a combination of your favorite hot sauce and melted vegan butter.

> 14 oz. (397 g) extra-firm tofu, prepared in advance
>   (see How-To, page 159)
> 1/4 cup (36 g) all-purpose flour or gluten-free flour of choice
> 1/4 cup (40 g) cornmeal
> 1/4 cup (15 g) nutritional yeast flakes
> 1 tablespoon sugar
> 1 1/2 teaspoons ground cumin
> 1 1/2 teaspoons salt
> 1 1/4 teaspoons garlic powder
> 1 1/4 teaspoons onion powder
> 1/2 teaspoon freshly ground black pepper
> 1/8 to 1/4 teaspoon ground cayenne
> 3/4 cup (180 ml) soy milk or other plant milk
> 1 tablespoon plus 2 teaspoons cornstarch
> 1/4 cup (60 ml) canola or other vegetable oil, divided

After the tofu has been prepared, chop each slice into cubes roughly an inch (2.5 cm) wide, and set aside.

Combine the flour, cornmeal, nutritional yeast, sugar, cumin, salt, garlic powder, onion powder, black pepper, and cayenne in a large, shallow dish and stir with a whisk. Combine the plant milk and cornstarch in a medium bowl and stir with a whisk until the cornstarch is mostly dissolved.

Heat 2 tablespoons of the oil over medium to high heat in a large frying pan, until a small test drop of the plant milk and cornstarch mixture sizzles upon contact. Using your hands or a spoon, briefly dip several tofu cubes at a time into the plant milk and cornstarch mixture, roll them in the flour mixture, and place in the pan. Fry the battered tofu cubes for 5 to 7 minutes, adding the remaining 2 tablespoons of oil if the pan becomes dry, and turning the cubes as each side becomes slightly browned.

Note: For additional flavor, drizzle 1 to 2 tablespoons of the remaining plant milk mixture onto the cooking tofu cubes, and then sprinkle 1 to 2 tablespoons of the remaining flour mixture onto the cubes, just before turning them a second time.

Kalamata Olive & Sun-Dried Tomato Hummus

Makes 3 1/2 cups (830 ml)

Blending umami with tartness, spice, and texture, this topping walks hand-in-hand with the Caramelized Onion and Garlic Waffles (page 102) or the Naked Vegan Waffles (page 41).

> 2 cans (15 oz./425 g each) chickpeas, drained and rinsed
>   (about 3 cups/700 ml)
> 1/3 cup (80 ml) water
> 1/4 cup (60 ml) lemon juice
> 1/4 cup (60 ml) olive or other vegetable oil
> 1/4 cup (64 g) tahini (sesame seed butter)
> 2 tablespoons nutritional yeast flakes
> 2 medium cloves garlic
> 3/4 teaspoon salt
> 1/2 teaspoon chili powder
> 1/2 teaspoon paprika
> 1/16 to 1/8 teaspoon ground cayenne
> 1/3 cup (51 g) pitted Kalamata olives
> 1/4 cup (53 g) sun-dried tomatoes, preserved in olive oil or rehydrated

Process the chickpeas, water, lemon juice, oil, tahini, nutritional yeast, garlic, salt, chili powder, paprika, and cayenne in a food processor until smooth. Add the olives and sun-dried tomatoes, and pulse for 2 to 3 seconds at a time until pieces are the desired size.

If you don't have a food processor, mash the chickpeas, crush the garlic, and chop the olives and sun-dried tomatoes by hand. Then mix all ingredients in a medium bowl until well blended.

Note: For an added twist, top the hummus with a swirl of the reddish-hued olive oil from the sun-dried tomatoes, alongside a dusting of paprika and a fresh lemon wedge.

Pickled Mango Tahini

Makes 1 1/2 cups (350 ml)

This savory vegan waffle topping recipe is inspired by a Middle Eastern chickpea dish. It has a rich, somewhat tangy, intense flavor. You can spread it on waffles, or you can dip waffles into it like you would dip chips into hummus. Once you have a bottle of amba in your pantry, it may inspire other creative culinary endeavors. Pair with neutral waffles such as the Nice Rice-Teff Waffles (page 51).

> 1/2 cup (128 g) tahini (sesame seed butter)
> 1/2 cup (130 g) sliced pickled mango (amba)
> 1/2 cup (120 ml) lukewarm water
> 1/4 cup (60 ml) agave nectar or maple syrup
> 1/4 teaspoon ground sumac (optional)

Combine all ingredients in a food processor or blender. Process until mango pieces are chopped up very finely, or until mixture is completely smooth, depending upon your preference. Serve in a bowl for dipping or spreading, with a dusting of ground sumac on top.

Note: If you'd like the flavor to be a bit more intense, add 1 to 2 more tablespoons of pickled mango. If, on the other hand, it's a bit too tart for you, add 1 to 2 more tablespoons of agave nectar or maple syrup. If you can't find sumac spice, you can use a bit of paprika for a similar aesthetic effect, even though it doesn't have the tartness of sumac.

Ideas for Ultra-Quick Toppings

Is your time extremely limited, or are you preparing for a large event? Consider some of these vegan waffle toppings:

❖ any type of nut butter (e.g., peanut, almond, cashew), purchased pre-made or created at home with a food processor

❖ fresh, frozen, dried, or canned fruit, including pineapple or berries

❖ jam or preserves

❖ dried coconut

❖ vegan yogurt (can be mixed with fruit)

❖ granola

❖ trail mix

❖ any vegan cereal

❖ vegan cream cheese

❖ dairy-free ice cream

❖ vegan whipped toppings

❖ liquid sweeteners such as agave nectar and rice syrup

❖ store-bought hummus

❖ pre-made vegan chili

❖ guacamole

❖ salsa

❖ beans with herbs and spices added—for example, chickpeas in a pre-made Indian spice blend, or vegan refried beans with cumin and cilantro

❖ vegan chocolate chips (may be melted to make a sauce)

❖ rice with spices, or incorporated into a pre-made vegan cooking sauce

❖ spicy tempeh

- ❖ crumbled veggie burger or veggie sausage
- ❖ pizza or pasta sauce
- ❖ fruit or nuts mixed with maple syrup
- ❖ stir-fry vegetable mix with a pre-made sauce

Organizing & Hosting a Waffle Party

Once you have purchased a waffle iron and enjoyed a few recipes on your own, you may be eager to share delicious food with others. Vegan waffle parties can be an excellent way to connect with others, while acknowledging that reduction of animal product consumption supports friendlier, healthier, and more sustainable living.

Here I share some important things we've learned over the years, in hopes that your waffle parties are wildly successful right from the start. If you've already thrown many food-related parties, some of the following material will be old hat for you. However, waffles do require some special considerations because they're prepared on the spot, and there are important things to keep in mind if you're reaching out to both vegan and non-vegan guests.

What is a Waffle Party?

A waffle party is a festive and stomach-filling social event where waffles are served, preferably hot off the iron, with delicious toppings. It can be a relatively simple gathering with just a few friends, or it can be an extravagant production with dozens of guests. The only major items needed are a waffle maker, a vegan waffle recipe, waffle making ingredients, and some hungry friends who are willing to bring vegan waffle toppings and have fun.

Why an Event Featuring Vegan Waffles?

The vegan waffle is especially well-suited for building awareness and increasing interconnectedness. Here are some of the most important reasons to host and enjoy a vegan waffle party:

❖ Even with excellent resources on delicious vegan cupcakes, cookies, and other vegan foods, there's still a great need to build awareness that baked goods can be done without dairy and eggs.

❖ Waffles are broadly recognized and enjoyed, and vegan ones often taste even better. Many people are especially surprised to learn that waffles can be vegan—then they wonder, "If waffles, why not other baked goods?"

❖ Waffles are fun, delicious, and versatile—they can function as a main course for breakfast, brunch, lunch, or dinner, or they can serve as a novel dessert.

❖ Waffles are inexpensive and relatively easy to make. Creating a batch of batter is simpler than preparing a complex 2- or 3-dish meal.

❖ Asking guests to bring vegan waffle toppings gives them an easy way to participate and share. For non-vegan friends, concocting a topping can be less intimidating than making a full vegan dish.

❖ Those just learning the benefits of a plant-strong diet and lifestyle may feel a bit overwhelmed at first. Most of us have been there ourselves. Vegan waffle parties offer a fun and gentle way to enjoy food while altering common misconceptions. For example, an array of toppings illustrates that there really are many plant-based food options available.

History of the Waffle Party

For decades, one of the world's most fascinating foods was viewed merely as a breakfast item. In 1998, this misconception ended. In our small apartment in Baltimore, Maryland, creative forces converged to catalyze what is now believed to be the world's longest-running annual waffle party.

Each year, guests and hosts have continued to expand the boundaries of waffle topping possibilities, going far beyond traditional maple syrup. They have discovered that waffles can harmonize with ingredients including spices, veggies, curries, and tofu. Creative guests bring toppings they have always desired to try on a waffle. In the company of other gastronomic pioneers, they freely experiment and achieve new levels of culinary excitement.

In 2001, we moved to Pittsburgh, Pennsylvania, continuing the tradition there. In November of that year, responding to a question on the word "waffle," The Word Detective (word-detective.com) noted that the earliest known mention of the word in English (1744) includes a "waffle frolic." This was apparently an event centered around making and eating waffles. It is possible that similar events could have occurred even earlier in other parts of the world. Upon discovering this a few years later, we were excited to realize that we may have revived an almost-forgotten festivity.

As we gained awareness of the impacts of our diets and lifestyles, the waffle party became vegetarian and then vegan. In May 2008, several cities participated in the first Global Vegan Waffle Party. Some websites even declared a new holiday: World Vegan Waffle Day, the Saturday right before the last Monday in May. The vegan waffle party "home base" moved to Portland, Oregon in 2013, and the tradition continues.

With your participation, the positive energy and awareness will continue to expand. More and more people across the globe will recognize that delicious baked goods do not require eggs or dairy.

Developing a Vision

In *The Seven Habits of Highly Effective People*, Stephen Covey advises, "Begin with the end in mind." Such a mindset helps to ensure that you create the event you really want. There are many possible ways to throw a waffle party, and many reasons for throwing one. Here are a few questions to ask yourself as you begin to plan:

❖ For what reasons do you wish to throw a waffle party? In other words, what is the primary purpose of the event? Some possible reasons include: just for fun, getting to know new people, introducing others to vegetarianism and veganism, impressing friends with your creativity and cooking acumen, or getting to know other vegetarians and vegans in your community.

❖ Who is your audience and how large is the event going to be? Both may be driven by the answer to the first question regarding purpose. These answers may also depend upon the resources you have available, including space, time, equipment, and money.

❖ How long would you like the party to last? You might decide to have an open house for several hours, or you might wish to limit your event to 2 or 3 hours.

❖ How much time would you like to spend visiting with guests? If you're having a large party, the waffle baking alone may take significant time and effort.

The answers to these questions will help you to organize the event in a way that generates the desired results. For example, if a primary purpose is to get to know new people, and you want to have at least 2 hours to chat with guests, you'll probably want to minimize the time you spend baking waffles in the kitchen during the party. On the other hand, if your primary purpose is to show off how delicious vegan food can be, and to introduce others to delicious vegan food, then you may end up spending much more time baking—but you'll still enjoy it because it fits your purpose for throwing the party.

As you develop your vision, remember that it needs to be fun for you as well as your guests. If you feel like you're making the party bigger or more complex than you can handle, consider simplifying it or asking for more help. If you're not having fun, your guests will sense it and they won't have a good time either. That defeats the purpose of having a party.

After several years of throwing annual waffle parties, we reworked our vision because we weren't satisfied with some aspects of previous events. We enjoyed the excitement and variety of a large crowd, and I really enjoyed baking the waffles, but we also wanted more time to visit with guests. Most people would show up during the first hour or two, during which time I was quite busy baking waffles. By the time I finished, most of the guests had already been there a few hours and had begun to leave. That gave me little time to visit.

Clarifying our vision for the party led us to some innovative solutions. Using an online event planning and invitation site, I designated 2 arrival times spaced 2 hours apart (6:00 PM and 8:00 PM), with each "shift" allowing around 20 people. I spent just under an hour making fresh waffles at each of those times. In between, I turned off the irons and took time to mingle with guests, sample toppings, and enjoy other aspects of the party. This provided a better balance for us.

As you define what you want, consider developing a title or theme for your party. If you're artistically inclined, you can even create a logo or theme song! For example, one of our parties was entitled "Vegan, Green and Delicious" because we wanted to emphasize the environmental benefits of a vegan lifestyle. We also took other steps to make the party more ecologically friendly. If you really enjoy chocolate, you might host a party where guests bring vegan waffle toppings containing cocoa. If you like spicy foods, your gathering might feature an array of southern Indian toppings. The possibilities are literally endless.

Food Preparation Tips

For many types of parties, all the food can be prepared in advance. Waffles, however, are best served hot out of the iron. Baking a fresh vegan waffle for each guest is part of what makes a waffle party special. This requires a few logistical considerations. You can take steps to minimize the amount of time guests must wait for food, increase the speed with which you create waffles, or both.

Test drive the recipes in advance

To reiterate a key point, always try the recipes you plan to use in advance, even if it means halving each recipe so you can bake 1 or 2 test waffles. If time allows, bake a test waffle on each iron you plan to use. This will lessen the odds of a waffler's worst nightmare: a severe sticking or charring incident. You can freeze any surplus test waffles for later consumption.

Prepare wet & dry batter portions beforehand

It can be difficult to focus on details like measuring ingredients during the party, while you're also hosting and talking to guests. To increase baking efficiency and maintain calmness during your event, measure out the wet and dry batter portions in advance. If you're making more than one kind of waffle, label each jar or container of wet ingredients and its corresponding bowl of dry ingredients so you know which portion goes with which. If you do this the night before the party, keep the wet mixture portion in a sealed container in the refrigerator and the dry mixture portion in a covered bowl on the counter.

Yeast-raised and flaxseed-containing recipes will have 3 separate portions. Yeast-raised recipes will include the following: the yeast-raised portion that is left to rise for several hours, the additional liquid ingredients added shortly before baking, and the baking soda or baking powder that is dissolved in the liquid just before adding the liquid to the yeast-raised portion.

For flaxseed-containing recipes, keep the flaxseed separate until mixing all the portions together. Its binding power and thickness can increase when sitting in liquid for extended periods, which may increase the odds of waffles sticking to the iron. Adding more water afterwards may resolve this, but not always.

An hour or two before baking, take the premixed wet portion out of the refrigerator so it has time to warm slightly. Then, within 15 minutes of baking, give the wet ingredients a good shake or stir if needed, and mix together the portions according to the recipe's directions.

To maximize waffle-making efficiency while minimizing waffle batter waste, consider preparing batches that will make roughly 8 waffles each. This generally means doubling a recipe. Smaller batches result in more frequent mixing during the party, which takes time and effort. Larger batches may result in more mixed but unused batter at the end. If you're hosting a large party and don't want to do all the advance batter preparation on your own, consider hosting a small "batter prep party" with a few friends or roommates the night before the event. Remind them to bring measuring cups and spoons, or have extras on hand.

The following photos illustrate premixed wet and dry ingredients for several batches of vegan waffles. The small labels have abbreviations indicating each type of waffle, to ensure proper matching of wet and dry portions. Note the reuse of beverage and food containers.

Premixed wet ingredients for several batches of waffles

Premixed dry ingredients for several batches of waffles

Secure a second waffle iron

Another way to increase cooking capacity is to borrow or purchase a second waffle iron. Suppose a single iron bakes a waffle large enough for 1 person in 4 minutes, and it takes an additional 2 minutes to remove a waffle from the iron, allow the iron to fully reheat (necessary for some but not all irons), and pour batter for the next waffle. Excluding any time needed to prepare fresh batches of batter, your maximum capacity will be around 10 waffles per hour. If you're inviting a large number of people, this may not be acceptable. Being able to bake 2 waffles at once may give you the necessary capacity.

Running multiple irons becomes easier with practice, and it requires a system for keeping track of multiple cooking times. If your waffle irons are identical or bake at roughly the same speed, it will simplify things because you can establish a rhythm with which you start and remove waffles—either pouring batter for both and removing both at the same time, or staggering them. As I explain under "Waffle Irons and Other Essential Equipment" (page 34), two separate irons with decent wattages will give you more baking capacity than one iron that dilutes a similar wattage over a larger area.

Cut waffles into quarters

If obtaining more irons is not an option, but you're still concerned about guest wait time, you can encourage a slower waffle consumption rate. Simply divide each fresh waffle into quarters with a pizza cutter. This allows several guests to start eating at once, instead of one guest getting a whole waffle while everyone else continues to wait. By the time guests finish topping their waffle quarters and eating them, another batch is ready. This approach also makes it easier to try different toppings without mixing incompatible ones, e.g., savory toppings on one quarter, and sweet toppings on the next.

Have a two-shift event

Yet another possibility, mentioned earlier, is to decrease the speed at which your guests arrive by offering more than one arrival time, with an attendance cap placed on each (see "Developing a Vision," page 169). This will avoid a large rush of hungry guests all at once, and it will give you space to breathe and mingle between arrival times.

Host a DIY waffle baking adventure

If you want to decrease the time you spend baking during the party, you can allow guests the opportunity to make their own waffles. However, this is wise only if you have space for more cooks in your food prep area, and only if you have at least one extra backup iron in case of a sticking incident. Your guests won't know the nuances of your waffle iron, and a failure to spray oil on the grids properly or an attempt to open the iron far too soon can create a mess and an extended wait.

Create an emergency backup if needed

If you realize that you're going to have more attendees than you can manage with your cooking capacity, and none of the above strategies will do the trick, there is a last resort: serving reheated frozen waffles alongside your fresh homemade waffles. In my opinion, frozen vegan waffles will never quite stack up to freshly baked ones, but some are still pretty tasty—especially with toppings. Just heat up a few store-bought waffles in the toaster while you're also baking fresh waffles. Depending on your schedule, you could also bake some homemade "backup waffles" a day or two before, put them in the freezer, and reheat them as needed during the party. See more on storing and reheating waffles on page 21.

Vegan Party Etiquette

When you're inviting people with a range of eating preferences and asking them to bring food, you can avoid several potential pitfalls.

Catering to a mix of lifestyles

Throwing parties for a combination of vegan and non-vegan individuals can be great fun, as it encourages togetherness and allows many people to try something different. However, there are a few things to keep in mind.

First, provide guests with advance notice regarding the guidelines for ingredients, and be as clear as possible. This will help to prevent embarrassing and uncomfortable situations. Be prepared for the possibility that some guests may still overlook the guidelines, especially if they're already inundated with email and have a busy schedule.

If one of your guests brings a non-vegan item, you face the balancing act of making them feel as welcome as possible while maintaining a comfortable environment for your vegan guests. You might start by thanking them for bringing a dish, letting them know they made an honest oversight, and explaining the need to maintain a comfortable and safe environment for all your guests. You might discreetly offer to store their topping out of sight in the refrigerator for them until they're ready to go home, or place it on a side table with a label very clearly indicating its non-vegan ingredients. It's up to you.

The first year our waffle party was vegetarian, a friend who had attended in previous years overlooked this change and accidentally brought a flesh-based dish. He was obviously embarrassed, but we still thanked him for bringing it, placed it on one of the side tables for guests who weren't vegetarian, and made sure it was labeled very clearly. You could take a similar approach with a dish containing egg or dairy.

Secondly, clearly inform your vegan guests if you are also having non-vegan guests, and vice-versa. This lets your vegan guests know to be on the lookout for non-vegan items brought by accident. While as a host you should do your best to check for such items, it can be difficult to spot everything. Some people may wish to decline your invitation if there's a chance of an occasional non-vegan dish.

Thirdly, in your invitation materials, you may wish to emphasize that while all the food will be vegan, everyone is welcome regardless of their current eating habits. Our invitations often state, "You don't have to be vegan, but the topping you bring does." This helps to set an inclusive tone and implies that guests will be expected to embrace the same attitude. It also addresses the previous point, by letting your vegan guests know that non-vegans may be present.

Being mindful of other dietary requirements

When planning your party, you'll need to decide how many types of requirements you can comfortably accommodate, so that you can announce them up front. For example, are you planning to provide gluten-free waffles, soy-free waffles and toppings, or even a raw vegan alternative to waffles? Will some or all of your items also be organic? It's entirely up to you how inclusive you wish to be. If a few of your guests have allergies to common ingredients that aren't in the waffles, but that may be in some of the toppings, you can ask guests to label toppings with their name, the dish name, and the ingredients. This way, anyone who must avoid specific items can see what's in each dish and track down its creator with any questions.

Making it easy for guests to get to know one another

Name tags sound like a no-brainer, but I don't see them at many parties, and we often forget them at ours. This is especially important if you've invited guests from your regular "vegan food outing group" as well as guests from other settings. Encouraging everyone to add something creative to their name tag, such as their favorite flavor, can serve as an ice breaker.

Welcoming both positive & constructive feedback

When hosting an event with a social consciousness theme, you'll naturally attract some guests who set high standards for themselves and for others. Some may consider it their ethical duty to inform you of things that could be improved. Even when you've done your best, they will find something you've overlooked—perhaps you could have avoided a few paper plates, or perhaps you could have made sure all the drinks were organic. Maybe you could have asked your non-vegan neighbor not to wear a leather outfit to the event.

The best I can suggest is to be prepared for such things and recognize that you will never make everyone 100% happy. Nonetheless, you may profoundly impact some of your guests, save many lives, provide inspiration, and create more change than you realize. This can be difficult to measure, but it will likely dwarf any seemingly negative energy you happen to receive.

Remind yourself of your primary purpose for hosting the event. For example, is it to create a certain appearance of yourself, or is it to have fun while improving the world? With that in mind, embrace constructive feedback that may help you to fulfill your purpose even better next time. On the other hand, discard feedback that doesn't help to you achieve your purpose.

At the same time, don't get so caught up in hosting a perfect event that you overlook all the little compliments you receive. Because hosting often involves spotting and fixing anything that may be wrong or out of place, it can be easy to focus on what's going wrong and lose track of what's going right. Focus on the parts that seem to be the most fun for everyone, and ask yourself how you can create even more of that next time.

Physical Setting Logistics

The unique nature of the waffle party also demands some special considerations regarding physical layout. Following are ideas for maintaining a comfortable atmosphere for everyone.

Entryway

If you're going to be cooking waffles in the kitchen as guests are still arriving, you won't be available to answer the door, hang coats, and so on. Thus, you can use signs to direct people where to put their shoes and coats, or you might ask a friend to help answer the door during the initial rush.

Dining room

Visualize yourself as a hungry and thirsty guest who has just arrived. Take a few moments to mentally run through the actions you would take. For example, what do you look for as you prepare to eat and drink, and in what order? Prior to grabbing a waffle, you'll probably look for a plate and a fork, and possibly a napkin. Hopefully these items will be conveniently nearby and won't require pushing through a crowd or standing in line again. After grabbing a waffle, you'll be seeking toppings, and then possibly something to drink. You can do this "pretend you're a guest" visualization as you're planning, and again the day of the party as you're getting everything set up.

One dining room item in particular will save you significant effort if you plan to have a large crowd. Place the freshly baked waffle set-out and pick-up point as close to the waffle irons as you can, while still maintaining enough space around you to bake safely and comfortably. This way you don't have to squeeze through a crowded room to put the fresh waffles on the table.

Kitchen

If you have a small kitchen or are expecting enough guests to require running multiple waffle irons, you may need to take additional steps to ensure that your kitchen remains an efficient and safe working space.

Beyond possibly having the waffle set-out and pick-up point nearby, do what you can to minimize kitchen traffic, at least in the space immediately surrounding where you're baking. Guests crowding near the waffle irons can pose a potential safety hazard. Keep as many of your food and drink supplies as possible in other rooms. Utilize coolers for drinks and ice so that guests don't need to visit the refrigerator. You don't want anyone, including yourself, getting a burn or having a large bowl of batter spilled on them. If you have a very small kitchen with a back door, you may wish to place a sign outside redirecting people to the front door.

Because waffle irons are high-wattage appliances, determine the limits of your house or apartment's electrical system before running multiple irons at once. One year we faced the embarrassment of having the lights and stereo go out during our party, when I attempted to turn on the microwave while waffle irons were running. Apparently, I had plugged too many items into the same circuit. After I switched one of them to a different outlet, all was fine. In kitchens with older wiring, running too many high-wattage items might even present a safety hazard.

If your party is in the summer, you may wish to place a fan in a kitchen window to exhaust heat, moisture, and the smoke that the hot cooking oil can sometimes produce. This is especially important if you're using a few waffle irons at once. Even if you're hosting an event during colder weather, have a fan readily available near a window or door that's easy to open if necessary.

Keeping It Environmentally Friendly

Introducing others to creative vegan food can benefit the environment by reducing animal-based agriculture. However, you don't want to cancel out any positive impacts by generating a lot of waste. This is particularly likely when you're having a large party, because the idea of having a pile of dishes to wash can make the immediate convenience of disposables especially tempting. Below are a few tips for minimizing any negative ecological impacts of your party. Keep in mind that you'll also be setting a good example for others.

❖ Turn off waffle irons when not used for extended periods.

❖ If you don't have enough plates, cups, utensils, or cloth napkins, borrow some from a neighbor or friend, or consider having guests bring some of their own items.

❖ If you host large parties frequently, consider reusable, dishwasher-safe plates, cups, and utensils made of recycled plastic. Just like disposable dinnerware, it is lightweight, non-breakable, and stackable in a minimal amount of space. By placing out several small bins for dirty plates, cups, and utensils, along with signs asking guests to scrape food into the trashcan before stacking their plates, you can reduce your cleanup efforts to loading and unloading the dishwasher a few times. We've done this for a number of waffle parties and have been pleased with the results.

❖ Because waffles with toppings can be messy, completely avoiding paper towels or napkins may be difficult at a larger party. In most cases, however, it doesn't take an entire paper towel or napkin to absorb a small amount of food from one's face or hands. Prior to the party, tear paper towels or paper napkins into halves or quarters. Someone can always grab a few more if they really need to.

Other Fun Ideas

Do you wish to provide an exceptionally creative experience for your guests? Here are some additional ways to make your vegan waffle party even more memorable and successful. Global Vegan Waffle Party hosts in other cities have already raised the bar by introducing some of these ideas:

❖ Bake waffles in conjunction with a bake sale for your favorite cause. If you have limited space where you live, ask to utilize a community organization's kitchen and dining area, or partner with a local business in a mutually beneficial way that helps them to draw customers.

❖ Host a vegan waffle party as a friendlier alternative to a regular non-vegan event that occurs in your area, e.g., a fish fry or non-vegan pancake breakfast.

❖ Suggest a vegan waffle party as an event for an existing local vegan or vegetarian group.

❖ Ask guests to share candidly what they liked most or least about the party, using an anonymous note card box.

❖ Encourage guests to vote on their favorite waffle topping and offer a prize to the winning chef.

❖ Convince your friends to host other vegan food events on adjacent weekends, creating an entire month of vegan-themed food parties.

❖ Ask local businesses if they would like to sponsor your event, contributing in return for ads placed on your event's web page or on materials displayed at your event. You can donate proceeds to a worthy cause.

❖ Offer other types of activities at your waffle party. This might include live entertainment, an educational film, or vegan food-making demonstrations.

❖ Use your imagination!

Inaugural Global Vegan Waffle Party Hosts & Cities

These individuals and groups have helped to get the party started. More are listed on the Wall of Hosts at waffleparty.com. There's still tremendous room for spreading awareness. Your participation can help to move it forward!

❖ Adrienne, Tualatin, OR

❖ Aletha at New World Dawn, Pontiac, MI, US

❖ Alexis and Waffle Frolic, Ithaca, NY, US

❖ Alisa F. at Go Dairy Free, Las Vegas, NV, US

❖ Allie C. and the Rogue Brunch Brigade, Baltimore, MD, US

❖ Amanda L. and the San Francisco Vegan Desserts Meetup, CA, US

❖ Amber M. and Café Green, Washington, DC, US

❖ Andrea and the Boston and Dorchester Vegan Mafias, Boston, MA, US

❖ Anika, Seattle, WA, US

❖ Autumn at Living Vegetarian, Old Fort, NC, US

❖ Avril S., South Wales, UK

❖ Beckert Babes Baking, East Haven

❖ Beth, Danbury, CT, US

❖ Betsy S. at Beer is Vegan, Durham, NC, US

❖ The Big Strawberry, Stoke-on-Kent, UK

❖ Billie D. at Wild Pure Heart, Braidwood, NSW, Australia

❖ Blakely S., Boston, MA, US

❖ Boston Vegan Waffle Party, Jamaica Plain, MA, US

❖ Brianne, Halifax, NS, Canada

❖ Bridget C., Canberra, ACT, Australia

❖ Brisbane Vegan Meetup, Queensland, Australia

❖ Christine "Peanut" Vardaros, Everberg, Belgium

❖ Café Evolution, Florence, MA, US

❖ Chelsi H., Jessup, PA, US

❖ Clark at Raven Facts, Berkeley, CA, US

❖ Cynthia and students at Cal Poly Pomona, US

❖ Dallas and the Animal Rights Coalition, Minneapolis, MN, US

❖ Dawn at Dawn's Custom Cakes, Cambridge, ON, Canada

❖ Dawn *et al.* at Waffle Shop, Pittsburgh, PA, US

❖ Derek and The Vegan Bus, Northampton, MA, US

❖ Destine, Hillcrest, Waikato, New Zealand

❖ Dylan Y., Norman, OK, US

❖ Earl B. and the Tokyo Vegan Meetup Group, Japan

❖ Earth Vegan Society, Greater Cumberland

❖ Edy H. at Vegan Recipes from the Heart, Aptos, CA, US

❖ Elaine V. and Vegas Veg* Meetup, Las Vegas, NV, US

❖ Elizabeth R., Grand Rapids, MI, US

❖ Emily at creATE, Ann Arbor, MI, US

❖ Emily G., Cambridge, MA, US

❖ Emma W., Cockeysville, MD, US

- Ena H., Munich, Bavaria, Germany
- Fair Grounds Coffeehouse, Iowa City, IA, US
- Feather at Vegan Around the World, Los Angeles, CA, US
- The Final Proof, Altrincham, Greater Manchester, England
- Freya Dinshah at the American Vegan Society, Malaga, NJ, US
- Garrett W. at Gee, Think, Plainfield, NJ, US
- Gary L. at Compassion4Animals, Falls Church, VA, US
- Go Vegan Santa Barbara, CA, US
- Haroula G., Athens, Greece
- Harvest Home Animal Sanctuary, Stockton, CA, US
- Heather D., Leah F., and the Fort Wayne Vegan/Vegetarians Group, IN, US
- Hollan H., Koloa, HI, US
- House of Pain Vegan Waffles, Montreal, QC, Canada
- Ida, Jackson Heights, NY, US
- Ida H., Noah L., VegOut NYC, and The Vegan Ideal, NY, US
- Jeanine H. and Delicious Donations, Braddock, PA, US
- Jeannie and the Chico Vegan Meetup, CA, US
- Jen at Devious Soybeans, Berkeley, CA, US
- Jennifer M. and Positively Veg*n Meetup, Fort Lauderdale, FL, US
- Jess at Cruelty Free WA, Fremantle, Western Australia
- Jessica C., Pendleton, SC, US
- Jessie Joy S., Boston, MA, US
- Joy Family, Albany, NY, US
- Judith at Big Raw and Vegan Blog, Klamath Falls, OR, US
- Karine Brighten Events and Berkeley Vegan Earth Day, Berkeley, CA, US
- Kassi W., Bryan, TX, US
- Kathryn B., Los Angeles, CA, US
- Katie P., Staten Island, NY, US
- Kerry S-D and Vegans of the Earth, Fort Ashby, WV, US
- Kiama Kitchen
- Kim M., Sebastopol, CA, US
- Krystal Leigh A., Toledo, OH, US
- Lily K., Las Vegas, NV, US
- Lise and Brian, Seattle, WA, US
- LOLA, CA, US
- Lolo R. at Sweat Records, Miami, FL, US
- Lori Anne A., Raw Passion Bistro, and the Dayton Vegan Challenge, OH, US
- Lou's Vegan Pancake Wedding Breakfast, Charleston, SC, US
- M.E. Matthews, Boston, MA, US
- Malek K., Korat (Nakhon Ratchasima), Thailand
- Margaret I., Cambridge, MA, US
- Maria and Counter Culture Collective, Santa Cruz, CA, US
- Marika, Richmond Hill, ON, Canada
- Marisa and James, Seattle and Duvall, WA, US
- Mary at Well on Wheels, Hamden, CT, US
- Meggie W. and Animal Allies Club, Orem, UT, US
- Melanie and John at The Wild Cow, Nashville, TN, US
- Meredith H., Vienna, VA, US
- Merri, Grosse Pointe, MI, US
- Michael S., Ithaca, NY, US
- Michaela, Canterbury, Kent, UK
- Michelle R., Fullerton, CA, US

- Mike R. at The Bunker, Guelph, ON, Canada
- Mimi T., Berkeley, CA, US
- Mommy and Me Brunch at Belly Sprout, Fullerton, CA, US
- The Noe Fellows, Herndon, VA, US
- Oh, Yeah! Ice Cream and Waffles, Pittsburgh, PA, US
- One Leaf Farm
- The Organic Sage, Hollywood, FL, US
- Pittsburgh Vegan Waffle Party Team (Dave, Jen, and friends), PA, US
- Portland Waffle Party Team (Dave, Megan, Sarah, and friends), OR, US
- Positively Veg*n, Ft. Lauderdale, FL, US
- Rachel at Thistle and Yellow Rose, Edinburgh, Scotland
- Rachel C., New Britain, CT, US
- Rachel H., Spring Hill, FL, US
- Raelene C., Richmond, CA, US
- The Renatos, Rockford, MI, US
- Rhett A., Jacksonville, FL, US
- S. Sanders, Vancouver, BC, Canada
- Sally and Triratna Buddhists, Nottingham, UK
- Sarah and Brian, Washington, DC, US
- Sarah B., Washington, DC, US
- Sarra B. and Mike L, Blatch Speakeasy & Seitan Shack O'Love, Seattle, WA, US
- Sinéad S., Vancouver, BC, Canada
- A Smexy Housewife, Harrisburg, PA, US
- Steven and Emerging Green Queers, Madison, WI, US
- Sharon D., Tavares, FL, US
- Sharonbelle, Tavares, FL, US
- Stevie's Waffle Wednesday on Saturday, Prancing Pony 909, and 909 Halcyon, Tempe, AZ, US
- Supercarrot at Vegan Review Podcast, Philadelphia, PA, US
- Susie "Bumblebee," Carrboro, NC, US
- Tammy, Torrance, CA, US
- TD's House of Gregan Waffles and Tattoo Parlour, Herndon, VA, US
- Toontz at Okara Mountain, Wisconsin, US
- Tuftz
- Valerie S., Maitland, FL, US
- Vegan Society of PEACE, Houston, TX, US
- Vegan Waffles Forever, Northern VA, US
- Vegas Veg Meetup, Las Vegas, NV, US
- Vegetarian Society of Tulsa Meetup, OK, US
- Wendy B. Vegan Waffle Happy Hour
- Wes A. and Vegans Rock Austin, TX, US
- Yaoh UK Vegfest, Bristol, UK
- Yvonne W., Wasaga Beach, ON, Canada

Glossary of Waffle Vernacular

If you plan to venture seriously into the realm of vegan waffles, it's important to know the lingo. Don't get caught being square at a round waffle party—or at any other waffle party, for that matter.

get yer grid on: Behave in a manner so indisputably cool that everyone wants to be around you, like when you're baking delicious vegan waffles.

Global Vegan Waffle Party: An annual event that utilizes vegan waffles, toppings, and house parties to promote awareness about vegan food and lifestyles.

off the grid: Term used to describe a successful and exciting waffle party.

Vaffeldagen: Waffle Day in Sweden, March 25.

vaffeldander: The small, crispy, burnt chips resulting from a waffle sticking to the iron badly.

wafflewich: A waffle treat made by sandwiching a topping between two waffle halves or quarters.

woffelganger: Variation of "doppelganger." A waffle that looks exactly like your own, possibly because another waffle party attendee used the same toppings as you did. Before accusing anyone of stealing your vegan waffle, make sure it's not just your woffelganger.

Wout!: Exclamation of excitement upon tasting the perfect waffle. It is a blend of "Woot!" and the last name of Cornelius Swartwout, who patented the first U.S. waffle iron on August 24, 1869.

Express Yourself

If you would like to help spread awareness about vegan food, consider hosting an event as part of the annual Global Vegan Waffle Party. Or, encourage your favorite local restaurant or other organization to sponsor one. See waffleparty.com for additional details. There you'll also find inspirational photos and highlights from others' events, links to promotional materials including emailable posters and website logos, and other information to help spread the word. Never underestimate the awesome power of a delicious vegan waffle!

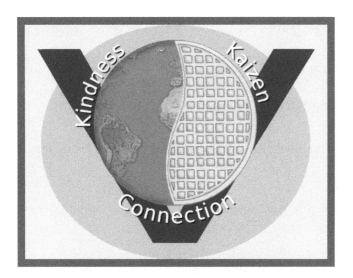

Acknowledgments

Many thanks to Jen, Megan, and Sarah for providing various forms of support, encouragement, and feedback, and for co-creating many wonderful waffle parties. Jo Stepaniak supplied expert feedback and motivation, inspired a few flavor combinations, and blazed the trail for vegan cookbooks like this one. The Pittsburgh Vegan Meetup group, Portland friends, annual Waffle Party attendees, and Vegetarian Summerfest crowd shared inspiration and knowledge. Rich Bjork assisted with proofing and inspired some creative concepts via his pastry chef wisdom. The vegan blogging community has helped to spread word about this concept, as have the hosts of vegan waffle parties in other cities and countries. They have also boosted my energy to complete this project.

The waffle recipe test team volunteers provided detailed feedback and suggestions that improved the text: Sallie Crick, Alice Doolittle, Emma Follender, Dani Goldman, Nir Goldman, Ida Hammer, Chris Holtz, Lauralee Holtz, Jen Joy, Marty Kinnard, Noah Lewis, Alan Lucas, Megan Martin, Sarah Martin, Benjamin Palmer, Tim Pearce, Brad Peniston, Anna Roberge, Heather Schall-Lucas, Ginny Silhanek, Rachael Smart, Ron Smart, Sally Stewart, Stephy Tang, Patrick Thompson, Lisa Tirmenstein, Christine "Peanut" Vardaros, Joanne Watral, and Portia Wu.

Vance Lehmkuhl kindly produced the current Global Vegan Waffle Party logo. Gary Crouth snapped the bio photo during one of our parties. Thanks to David Bennett and Isa Chandra Moskowitz for additional ideas on chopsticks. Isa and Terry's cupcake creativity increased my confidence that vegan waffles can also catalyze positive change. Hillary Rettig provided additional perspective on authoring and publishing. Pat Clark unknowingly catalyzed my first "blatantly vegan breakfast" experience, and Robbie Ali inspired me to question the status quo in new ways. Our neighbors and the Pittsburgh Cohousing Group sparked further thinking on how diet fits into sustainability. My parents and family sowed the seeds of caring, justice, compassion, and creative experimentation. Thanks to LeMew for helping to anchor the stacks of notes on the kitchen table. Many thanks to those of you who continue to spread the word through reviews, blog articles, social media shares, and other means. Deep gratitude to the higher energy that joins all of us on this journey, however you may perceive it.

About the Author

Since 1998, Dave has baked waffles for the world's longest-running annual waffle party. The original house party has evolved into the Global Vegan Waffle Party, with individuals, organizations, and businesses hosting events worldwide. Through waffleparty.com, Dave supports other hosts in spreading awareness about kinder, healthier, and more sustainable eating.

Dave also authored *The Vegan Chocolate Seduction Cookbook*, the self-empowerment guide for socially conscious people *Naked Idealism*, the touch-positive event how-to *The Snuggle Party Guidebook*, and several other self-help guides. Dave supports others in creating happier and more powerful lives via his strategic life consulting. He holds degrees in Psychology, Counseling, and Public Policy and Management, and is a Certified Life Coach. He has presented to various groups including the North American Vegetarian Society and American Mensa.

Dave enjoys composing music with social consciousness themes, beatboxing, gardening, hiking, and running in nature. To learn more about his other books, consulting, and music, visit davewheitner.com.

Dave skillfully removes a perfectly toasted vegan waffle.

Metric Measurement Methodology

This section includes more information than many readers will need, but I provide it for those who want the finer details. I originally created most of the recipes in this book using U.S. cups volume measurements. To make the new edition friendlier for readers across the globe and for bakers who appreciate the greater consistency of weight measurements, I later added metric weight or volume measurements for most amounts greater than tablespoons. Here I describe some of the estimation and conversion methodology.

The liquid volume-to-volume conversions were generally the most straightforward. In most cases, I simply used online conversion tables.

The non-liquid volume-to-weight (e.g., cups to grams) conversions required more effort. I took fresh volume samples and recorded the weights to obtain the grams per cup densities for the following items: ingredients whose densities can vary greatly depending upon one's personal measuring style, including most flours, grains, and seeds utilized like flours; other ingredients I keep on hand and/or use regularly; and ingredients for which I could not find density data in online food databases or on food packaging nutrition labels. When I came across online or label sources that differed, I averaged them, used the source that seemed more reputable, or re-obtained the item to weigh myself, depending upon the degree of difference.

Following are more details on how I did the volume-to-weight conversions for most of the flours and several other ground or powdered solid ingredients. First, I settled upon a volume measuring technique that approximates my measuring style and yields reasonably consistent results: the stir, scoop, and level technique described under "Measurement of flour" (page 15). Using this technique, I then took multiple volume measurements of each ingredient, weighing each sample. I used the average to calculate a grams per cup density for that ingredient. I then used that density to convert cups to grams in recipes using that ingredient.

The density of some ingredients varied significantly depending upon the size of the measuring cup used. For example, buckwheat scooped 1 cup at a time had an average density of around 150 g/cup, while buckwheat scooped 1/4 cup at a time had an average density of around 120 g/cup. This makes sense because the weight of the flour upon itself in a larger cup will cause it to pack more tightly. So, in the case of a recipe calling for 1 1/4 cups of buckwheat, I calculated the total weight using the higher density for the first cup and the lower density for the remaining 1/4 cup. For ingredients where the density variance across cup sizes was not substantial, I didn't use different densities for different cup sizes in conversions.

Finally, I tested a sample of recipes representing different types of waffles, using the new metric weight conversions rather than the original volume measurements. The waffles turned out as expected, suggesting that the conversions are reasonably accurate.

While I put significant effort into providing accurate metric conversions, there is undoubtedly some degree of error. The limitations include the following: I was unable to retest every recipe, my original volume measurement techniques likely had some inconsistency across recipes, and different brands of the same ingredient can vary in milling technique and thus density. Nonetheless, I believe the conversions are an improvement over volume measurements alone. I hope this addition adds value for you if you prefer metric measurements, or if you appreciate the greater consistency of using weights for baking ingredients like flour. I want you, your family, and your friends to enjoy the best vegan waffles possible.

Index